LIVING
Writers

A new approach to English

POETS

Mick Gowar
and
Dennis Hamley

Nelson

Thomas Nelson and Sons Ltd
Nelson House Mayfield Road
Walton-on-Thames Surrey
KT12 5PL UK

51 York Place
Edinburgh
EH1 3JD UK

Thomas Nelson (Hong Kong) Ltd
Toppan Building 10/F
22A Westlands Road
Quarry Bay Hong Kong

Thomas Nelson Australia
102 Dodds Street
South Melbourne
Vic 3205 Australia

Nelson Canada
1120 Birchmount Road
Scarborough Ontario
M1K5G4 Canada

First published by Thomas Nelson and Sons Ltd 1992

ISBN 0-17-439680-5
NPN 9 8 7 6 5 4 3 2 1

Printed in Hong Kong.

The authors and publishers wish to thank the following who have kindly given permission for the use of copyright material:

John Cotton for 'The Leg of a Pig' by John Cotton from Two by Two by John Cotton and Fred Sedgwick, Mary Glasgow Publications;

Faber & Faber Ltd for 'Rondeau Redouble', 'Reading Scheme', 'Waste Land Limericks', 'Tich Miller' and 'My Lover' from Making Cocoa for Kingsley Amis by Wendy Cope, 1986;

John Mole for 'The Three-legged Pig';

Oxford University Press for 'The Butcher', from The Onion Memory by Craig Raine, 1978; and 'A Martian Sends a Postcard Home' and 'In the Kalahari Desert' from A Martian Sends a Postcard Home by Craig Raine, 1979;

Peters Fraser & Dunlop Ltd. on behalf of the author for 'The Indentification' from Gig by Roger McGough, Jonathan Cape, 1973; 'Tramp, tramp, tramp', 'Bars are down', Prayer to St. Grobianus, 'A Cautionary Calendar' and 'First Haiku of Spring' from Melting Into the Foreground by Roger McGough, Jonathan Cape; and 'Bottom' from Pillow Talk by Roger McGough, Puffin Kestrel, 1990;

Vernon Scannell for 'A Case of Murder', 'Nettles', Growing Pain' and 'A Partial View';

Anthony Thwaite for 'A Haiku Yearbook' from Poems 1953-01988. © Anthony Thwaite;

Every effort has been made to trace all the copyright holders but if any have been inadvertently overlooked the publishers will be pleased to make the necessary arrangement at the first opportunity.

Photo Credits
Barnaby's Picture Library: Pages 63, 66, 89.
Camera Press: Page 84.
Faber and Faber Ltd Publishers: Pages 40 *Mark Chichester-Clark*, 60 *Mark Gerson*, 42.
Mansell Collection: Page 33.
Roger McGough: Pages 22, 25.
Robson Books: Page 80.
Visual Arts Library: Pages 47 Edward James Foundation © ADAGP, Paris and DACS, London 1993, 64 © DACS, 1993.
Rene Magritte: Page 47 Le Reproduction Interdite 1937
Pablo Picasso: Page 64 The Three Musicians.

Contents

Roger McGough

Wendy Cope

Craig Raine

Vernon Scannell

General introduction

Living Writers is intended mainly for fourth and fifth year students in secondary schools and their teachers. The main purpose of the series is to develop students' understanding of the process of writing and to improve their own skills in all aspects of English. It does this firstly by providing first-hand accounts by prominent writers on how, why and what they write, based on more than thirty hours of taped interviews, secondly by giving students a taste of the authors' writing and thirdly by a variety of reading, writing and discussion activities.

Living Writers comprises three books: *Novelists, Poets* and *Dramatists*. Each book helps students to examine the work and writing processes of four writers in that genre. The authors have deliberately chosen writers of quality who are accessible and may already be known to secondary students.

In this the third of the *Living Writers* books, four poets in interview give accounts of their lives, their works and how and why they write. Roger McGough, Wendy Cope, Craig Raine and Vernon Scannell provide us with insights into their writing. Students are led, through understanding and empathy with these poets in particular, to think about and develop an understanding of the craft of poetry in general. This is aimed at improving their own reading and writing. The assignments emphasise the links between the attainment targets of speaking and listening, reading and writing through small group discussion, collaborative and individual reading and individual and collaborative writing. They aim to help the student in some way to share the experience of each poet.

The four poets and their work are shown in context, both in terms of what they say in the interviews about what has influenced them and in terms of their place in the wider area of literature.

Each *Living Writers* book contains:

- Interviews with four living writers;
- Background information on the writers and their work;
- Extracts from the writers' work;
- Assignments – practical suggestions for work with students in the classroom;
- Information about movements and techniques in literature with suggestions for selecting further books and resources;
- Teachers' introduction to the assignments;
- Students' self-assessment sheet;
- Section on how to provide your own 'Living Writers'.

Living Writers has been developed to be of direct relevance to students facing the challenges of Key Stage 4 of the National Curriculum. It has been compiled by Mick Gowar and Dennis Hamley. Both are well-known writers of books for young people and visit many schools, libraries and colleges to give readings and talks and to lead workshops. Mick Gowar, as well as writing stories, is a poet. Dennis Hamley is also County English Adviser for Hertfordshire.

Living Writers provides not only useful source material but also practical support for teachers and students exploring the wider possibilities offered by the revised criteria for GCSE in English and English Literature.

ORAL WORK

This book may be used as a model for conducting your own interviews, either with living writers (see page 108) or with readers (class members, teachers, librarians, parents) following the basic pattern:

- Early encouragement and stimulus to write and read?
- Favourite or influential books, writers, type of writing?
- Specific details about one or two works: How/why did you come to write it? How/why did you come to read it?
- Particular writing skills you admire, e.g. form, metre, metaphor?
- 'Handy hints': practical tips to others on writing and reading?

Assignments emphasise group discussion work and the development of ideas, techniques and understanding.

WIDER READING

This book itself could be classified as 'wider reading'. Certainly it should stimulate a number of approaches to organised wider reading, e.g. finding out more about the writers or works mentioned by the writers who are interviewed; finding out more about the styles of writing, the forms and genres mentioned in the interviews. All of these could lead to the following.

SELECTION AND PREPARATION OF MATERIAL

Students select and prepare stories, poetry and dramatic writing for anthologies or for performance.

PERSONAL WRITING

Numerous suggestions are offered to stimulate and develop students' own writing.

All the poets interviewed stress the importance to them of first learning the basic skills of poetry, not only for their development as writers but also to get the maximum enjoyment from poetry as readers. As Craig Raine put it: 'The lovely pleasures of rhyme and metre'.

Teaching and learning prosody can be a slog, albeit a necessary one. The challenge to any teacher is how to make it less of a chore. The first stage is obviously to feel confident and on top of the subject, and a superb book for both the teacher and the most able pupils is Vernon Scannell's *How to Enjoy Poetry* (Piatkus). For a more detailed and academic approach, the books in the Methuen *Critical Idiom* series are excellent, especially *The Stanza* by Erns Haublein, *Metre, Rhyme and Free Verse* by G S Fraser and *The Sonnet* by John Fuller.

Equipped with the basic information, students can undertake practical tasks such as collecting together an anthology of poems grouped not around theme but around basic forms (see page105); constructing a poetry-display or putting together a handbook (for the use of others as much as for themselves) on basic forms illustrated with examples; reorganising some resources – photocopies of single poems, etc. – into a classification based on forms.

If necessary, work from a simple check-list, e.g:

TYPES OF RHYME:

Rhyme Royal
Traditional ballad stanza
Terza Rime
Ottava Rima
Heroic couplet
Heroic quatrain
End rhyme
Internal rhyme
Masculine rhyme
Feminine rhyme
Half-rhyme
Blank verse
Free verse
Alliteration
Assonance

LYRIC FORMS:

Sonnet
Villanelle
Rondeau
Ballade
Sestina
Triolet

NARRATIVE FORMS:

Ballad
Saga
Epic
Allegory
Satire

OTHER STANZA FORMS:

Haiku
Tanka
Ghazal
Limerick
Clerihew

As can be seen in the interviews, poets get a lot of stimulation and enjoyment from writing in strict form. Students should be encouraged to try some of the less fiendish forms, like haiku and tanka (a good starting place as these teach the basic disciplines of syllable count and line length), limericks, couplets, possibly even triolets. Setting a class or group the task of writing the more complex forms such as the sestina is, however, an act of brutality! Brian Powell's *English Through Poetry Writing* (OUP) is a particularly good source of ideas for this sort of writing exercise.

STUDENTS' OWN VERSE

Creative writing, poetry writing – whatever name you give it – is well-established as part of the primary and lower secondary curriculum and, thanks to GCSE, becoming more established with older pupils too. Many teachers are somewhat reticent to undertake this sort of activity, often unnecessarily so. Perhaps calling such classes 'workshops' has created too much of an aura of separateness and specialness around what are, after all, nothing more than English lessons. Some hesitate because they feel very reluctant to 'judge', 'evaluate' or even comment on *poems*; few, if any, feel any such reluctance about evaluating a pupil's writing in prose.

There are many excellent books to help teachers with examples of starter exercises, pupil's work and tips on developing your own methods. Many arise from work in primary schools, but are nonetheless relevant and adaptable to older pupils. The following is a small selection:

Poetry In The Making – Ted Hughes, Faber

Does It Have to Rhyme? Sandy Brownjohn, Hodder & Stoughton

What Rhymes With Secret? Sandy Brownjohn

In Tune with Yourself – Jennifer Dunn, Morag Styles, Nick Warburton, CUP

Words Large As Apples – Teaching poetry 11-18, Mike Hayhoe and Stephen Parker, CUP.

Writing workshops in schools, organised by visiting poets, can be arranged through your regional arts board (see Your Own 'Living Writers' page 108) or the Poetry Society which runs the *Poets in Schools* scheme.

For further details contact the Education Officer, the Poetry Society, 22 Betterton Street, London WC2H 9BU.

SELECTING MATERIALS AND RESOURCES

The major problem to overcome when reviewing or updating materials and resources is finding out what is available. Poetry 0-16 – Morag Styles and Pat Triggs (Books For Keeps), is an excellent place to start. It provides an extensive book list divided into sensible and useful sections, helpful notes on each book, and a substantial section devoted to practical advice on teaching poetry.

POETRY FOR CHILDREN: A SIGNAL BOOKGUIDE – Jill Bennett and Aidan Chambers, Thimble Press. From the publishers of Signal magazine, Poetry books for children (4-16), a Signal bookguide by Brian Morse.

THE NEW WHERE'S THAT POEM – Helen Moris, Blackwell. A remarkable cross-index enabling you either to track down a particular poem, or to find a number of poems with a similar subject matter or theme.

POETRY ON CASSETTE OR RECORD An increasing number of cassettes and cassette/book packs are available on the market, although the companies do tend to produce cassettes either for younger children or adults.

Teacher's introduction to the assignments

The assignments are designed to take up points which are raised in the four interviews with poets. There is also an introductory assignment on the Poet's Language, intended to help students understand what the poets are saying, and improve their own writing in the process: a comparative assignment follows. The purpose of the assignments is to enable students

- to apply the poets' insights to their own reading;
- to use these insights to develop their own writing of poetry;
- to see how the poets concerned embody these insights in their own writing;
- through directed small group discussion and consequently their own writing, to communicate these insights and develop a critical vocabulary which will enable them to move to further study in literature.

The rationale behind the assignments is well expressed in the words of Michael Benton, quoted in *English for Ages 5-16* (The Cox Report; para. 7.22): 'the development of a methodology based upon concepts of reading and response rather than upon conventional, narrowly conceived ideas of comprehension and criticism'. It is also encapsulated in the identical wording of reading and writing criteria for GCSE English (paras 3.8.4 and 3.10.5): 'understand and appreciate choices which writers, including themselves, may make in language, structure and form to achieve the effects they want'.

The interviews are a sharing between the writer and the student: so, it is hoped, are the assignments. The words 'including themselves' are important.

The assignments themselves are specific and directed. However, they need not be ends in themselves; teachers will see plenty of other approaches which can lead on for them and still embody the principles stated above. It is hoped that English departments will use this book as a stimulus to develop resources for other poems and poets on the lines of these assignments, as well as extending these assignments.

Each assignment is based on the account of practice and method that is given by each poet. It seeks to enable the student to share the experience of each poet as directly as possible. From the starting point of the poet's testimony, each assignment goes on to develop activities which can be useful for the purposes of National Curriculum assessment at Key Stage 4. Although each assignment contains some individual work, directed small group discussion is integral. The assignments are conceived as essentially collaborative exercises. There is therefore considerable scope for them to be used as the basis for assessment of the speaking and listening profile component as well as for both reading and writing. On page 00 there is a list of Statements of Attainment which are addressed directly by activities in the assignments. These are placed at level 5 purely for example. Because all the activities are differentiated by outcome, no limit can be placed on the attainment levels that can be reached through them.

However, there are quite deliberately some assignments which may not be finished. The poetry assignments, like those of the other books, attempt to recapture the writers' experience. An essential part of that experience is that sometimes ideas don't lead to anything – or, if they do, it takes a long period of gestation in the mind. That is why, for example, Assignment 4 based on Wendy Cope's interview may peter out for many students during thought and discussion: the activity reappears as Assignment 3 based on Vernon Scannell's interview. For some students this may be a separate activity because they wrote a poem as a result of the earlier assignment and are starting again. For others, a train of thought started but not worked out for the earlier assignment might be reactivated. For yet others, no useable thought will emerge at all. There should be no penalty for this, as it is a common experience for many poets.

This, however, leads to a point about student writing which is often made and needs to be answered. Vernon Scannell once spent some time as a poet in residence in a new town. He did not find it an entirely good experience, as he shows in his book *A Proper Gentleman*. In it, he says:

'… children do not write poems … to make a poem, a real poem, demands intelligence, imagination, understanding, experience, and not least a knowledge of the craft.'

There is often a feeling that writing poetry is a different discipline from writing stories or plays: that there is something magical about it: that what non-poets have to say is therefore not worthwhile. Not many people are going to be poets anyway so what is the point of encouraging students to do something which they are, on almost every count, unsuited for?

There is obvious truth in this. It is very close to the 'cultural heritage' view of literature as a catalogue of milestones of great art which we survey in helpless admiration. Poetry, of course, often is great art; there are within it imperishable works which human beings are entitled to know, appreciate and regard as part of their possession and heritage. But what constitutes that appreciation? There are two ways to approach an answer which appeal to me. The first is that we tend to appreciate things better when we have direct experience of them and what went into them. The second is that in most areas of life, whatever the outcome, the process by which it is arrived at is similar. The difference is usually of degree and not kind. The thought process that Keats gradually outlines in his *Letters* or that Stephen Spender itemises quite closely in his essay *The Making of a Poem* is indeed mysterious. But it is a process which can be shared by most people – and is, indeed, at the heart of the view of the writing process developed in the National Writing project and the Language in the National Curriculum project. The real mystery comes with the greatness of some outcomes of this common process. For the purposes of understanding and appreciation, the importance is that we have access to how the writers did it. Besides which, even if some writing is better than other writing, it is no more valid as an expression important to the writer, nor has it any more right to be made and heard. The general recognition and acceptance for what it is and the criteria by which it becomes validated as something more than ephemeral is a different matter.

Football provides an analogy. There is only one Liverpool, only one Juventus. This does not make the thousands of Sunday League teams less worthwhile. Nor does it make the personal pleasure of the myriad players any less keen. But it does mean these players will watch Liverpool and Juventus with greater appreciation and knowledge because they have shared with those exceptional players a common experience and process in the actual playing of the game. And both sorts of player – international star or Sunday leaguer – keep training because they know that to remain good at the game they have to make its actions and rhythms as nearly instinctive and habitual to them as possible. Remember Jack Nicklaus's famous golfing remark about practising so much he got lucky. As in sport, so in poetry.

The rationale for the assignments

Unlike the other *Living Writers* books, there are six sets of assignments: a block for each poet and two general assignments. The four blocks of assignments based on individual poets contain some of their poems (including all those mentioned in the interviews) and in certain cases the work of other poets. There are also one or two relevant prose extracts. All are firmly based on the interviews and attempt to reproduce and share the experiences the poets are talking about.

It is important to note that while the interviews are separate, there are many linking themes. Chief among these is that all the poets had to learn their craft: they learnt it by reading other poets, writing like them until they found their own voice and had found out about, used and mastered a variety of forms. Poetry, then, is a craft to be learned and a long process. Another theme is that poems are not fully planned before they are written; when a poet starts s/he does not know what the 'clinching detail' of the end will be. At first sight there may seem a contradiction here; on the one hand the lonely slog till perfection is reached – on the other, the indiscipline of 'letting it all flow out', of 'making it up as you go along'. There is enough in the poets' testimony to resolve this seeming ambiguity – indeed, it is important that it is resolved. A prime aim of the assignments is to effect this resolution.

Work in any assignment is based on the particular poet – but all the work has general applicability to poetry. The order of assignments is such that they can be used separately, but there is an underlying sequence behind them and one or two assignments in particular can be seen as a continuation of the same process.

It is important to note that the first introductory assignment should be done before any of the others.

It is also important to note that the assignments (except the general assignments) are perhaps more tentative and less directive than those for the Novelists and Dramatists.

There is in these assignments a much greater emphasis on small group discussion focussing on particular works and particular points made in interview than in the other books. These discussions are not structured as closely as those in *Novelists* and, more particularly, *Dramatists*. Headings are given for the discussion to take place under and the device (which the authors hope will not prove irritating) of saying 'I don't know what you would have said but I …' is used merely to give some notion of where a discussion could lead. There are reasonable and rational insights to be made but there are no once and for all right answers and there is certainly no hint of the teacher/author saying 'Guess what's in my mind'.

There are several sorts of writing exercises. Those in the Roger McGough assignments lead to a communal poem and a 'calendar' poem which might be in haiku form. They are deliberately conceived as leading to performance because that is such a dominant theme in Roger McGough's interview. Another writing activity springs from his remarks about his family and the poems he wrote about them. Note that this is more of a critical than a creative assignment. Teachers might find a reading of *Meet my folks* by Ted Hughes will provide an interesting comparison – especially in the light of what Roger McGough says about how his poems were written.

The writing exercises in the Wendy Cope assignments refer directly to three elements in her interview. *The Reading Scheme* and the *My Lover/For I will consider my cat Jeoffrey* assignments aim at an aspect of her distinctiveness as a poet. *The Waste Land* Limericks exercise is a device to help with the reading and understanding of other poems as well as those of Wendy Cope or T S Eliot. There is no need to insist on student knowledge of *The Waste Land* – though if they want to read it afterwards and find that Wendy Cope's *Waste Land Limericks* have helped in this, then that is a great bonus.

The assignment based on her poem *Tich Miller* may not lead to any writing. Of course, it is hoped that it will; that the trains of thought Wendy Cope's account sets off may be vivid and quick in their effect. But they may not: the activity may lead to 'thoughts that lie too deep for words' and memories which give pain. Though students are working in groups, here the activity – even if elicited by talk – is in the end completely individual.

But the activity reappears in the Vernon Scannell assignments, so – if the assignments are done in order – the subconscious mind will have a period to work on the idea and, perhaps, provide a solution.

The assignments based on Craig Raine's interview lead to the most intensive and directed writing – and yet, at first sight, the most tangential. Use is made to the very specific points Craig Raine makes about his methods: his development of imagery, his borrowing from other art-forms and his reworking of prose passages (in *The Butcher* and In the *Kalahari Desert)*. For this reason the relevant prose passages are printed, as is also the joke which seems to be a very simple statement of his method in *A Martian Sends a Postcard Home*. The further example set – how other poets reached to a simple prose text – may seem frivolous. However, it is there to give the message that texts can be reacted to differently. The 'Martian' joke in the exercise is one that, despite its simplicity and banality, does have a number of interesting implications which reflect on particular features of the poems Craig Raine talks about.

The assignments based on Vernon Scannell's interview are more diffuse and reflective. The common theme of becoming a poet by looking at other poets is looked at more critically by this poet. More time is spent sorting out what he is actually saying because it may seem at first sight as if there is a contradiction between not writing poetry until he writes the truth and 'letting it all flow out'.

Here, careful examination of the draft of *Growing Pain* is important. The writing assignment can be a continuation of the Wendy Cope assignment four. The final assignment is a reading and discussion assignment and is deliberately placed at the end of the individual assignments to assert the potential power of poetry and a high view of the poet's worth and function. The poets have exhibited a wide range of feeling – light-hearted and deeply serious – but most has been in some way private even if it has touched on universal experience. The comparison of Vernon Scannell's modern poem *A Partial View* with Matthew Arnold's *Dover Beach* is meant to show students the power of poetry to articulate profound statements about our contemporary world; in Wilfred Owen's sense to 'warn'; to be, in Shelley's words, the statement of 'the unacknowledged legislator of the world'. The assignment is there to allow students to reflect more widely than the previous assignments have – and also, because of the *Dover Beach* reference, to understand the notion of continuity and tradition in poetry, which had been another of the major themes within the interviews.

The introductory assignment 'The Poets' Language' should be done before all other assignments because it will help give students experience of and feeling for words which will be important for all the activities to do with the separate poets. The Word Tree was developed over a long period by Jan Mark (interviewed in *Living Writers 1: Novelists*) and Mick Gowar, and is an ideal preparatory activity for any assignment where a sensitivity to words is required.

The comparative assignment takes up some of the questions to do with poetic form raised in the interviews and in the earlier assignments. The original versions of the poems by Austin Dobson, Thomas Hardy, Shakespeare and Wordsworth are at the end of this section (page 00). The poems can be photocopied and cut into lines so that the exercise can be done as a jigsaw (like the diamond games in *Living Writers 1*) or can be simply rewritten. Sequencing is always a useful activity. Here, the students have the clue of the set form they are reproducing, but there is also a large element of understanding of meaning. The students will actually be solving some of the problems of the original poet. They will not only have wrestled with form (and perhaps have internalised it), but they will have come closer to the poem than a mere first reading of it would have brought them. In some ways, sequencing can be described as 'surrogate writing'.

The other activity in the general assignment is more than a simple 'scissors and paste' job. The idea of the private anthology set out by form is conceived as an exercise in critical reading and 'scanning' texts quickly for information – in this case, identification of form. If the exercise means a use is found for old anthologies which might otherwise be thrown out then the authors are pleased.

There is a paradox at the heart of these assignments. Like all writing, poetry is a lonely activity, yet most of these tasks are done in groups. However, support from peers is important for most people. Where the process becomes exclusively individual is clearly signalled. Also, several tasks can be done either individually or collaboratively and which it is will often depend on the individual student. Teachers should be flexible here. There is, especially in the interview with Roger McGough, an emphasis on performance; this is why two activities are very strongly communal.

An important aim of all the *Living Writers* books has been to develop the writing community, a concept strong in both the National Writing Project and the Language in the National Curriculum project. Though the living writers are, when this book is used, only present by proxy, it is hoped that teachers themselves will join in this community and be seen as writers as much as the students. Teachers are writers: also, to share the writing process of the students (and be seen to) will not only help and raise the importance in the student's eyes of the whole activity: it will also help the teacher very much in identifying the assessment opportunities and understanding the nature of the assessment when it occurs by having a more immediate understanding of what is happening to the student.

An important function of these assignments is also either to prepare the way for or carry on the experience of visits by writers, perhaps under a scheme of a regional arts group such as the *Words* scheme of the Eastern Arts Association. Full details of how to organise such visits are on page 108.

Classroom and time management of these assignments is left to the individual teacher; the authors cannot legislate for all the many different situations schools are in. However, the assignments have been based on the assumption that English will be taught in double periods or in block timetables. The assignments do need a good run of time. However, careful organisation of groups should enable them to be attempted in shorter 35 to 40 minute periods.

National Curriculum Attainment Targets and Assessment

All the activities should provide evidence for National Curriculum Assessment in the three main Profile Components. On page 13 is a selection of statements of attainment which the assignments obviously address. These are set at level five, not because it is assumed that is the level which will be reached but because it provides a convenient example; versions of more or less complexity of the same language activity are expressed for all levels of attainment. English is a recursive subject which does not easily lend itself to the model of development in the way in which the levels of attainment are set out. Differentiation in all of the activities within the assignments is by outcome; all of the levels of attainment up to ten can be addressed by them.

Selected Attainment Targets: Attainment Level 5

SPEAKING AND LISTENING

- Give a well organised and sustained account of an event, a personal experience or an activity;
- Contribute to and respond constructively in discussion, including the development of ideas; in debate, advocate and justify a point of view;
- Use language to convey information and ideas effectively in a straightforward situation;

- Plan and participate in a group presentation.

READING

- Demonstrate, in talking and writing about a range of stories and poems which they have read, an ability to explain preference;
- Demonstrate, in talking about fiction, non-fiction, poetry, and other texts, that they are developing their own views and can support them by reference to some details in the text;
- Show in discussion that they can recognise whether subject matter in non-literary and media texts is presented as fact or opinion;
- Select reference books and other information materials and use organisational devices to find answers to their own questions;
- Show through discussion an awareness of a writer's choice of particular words and phrases and the effect on the reader.

WRITING

- Write in a variety of forms for a range of purposes and audiences, in ways which engage the interest of the reader;
- Produce, independently, pieces of writing showing evidence of the use of organisational devices, accuracy in sentence punctuation, including commas, and the setting out of direct speech, so as to clarify the meaning for the reader;
- Write in Standard English (except in contexts where non-standard forms are needed for literary purposes) and show an increasing differentiation between speech and writing;
- Assemble ideas on paper, or on a computer screen, or in discussion with others and show evidence of an ability to produce a draft from them and then to revise and redraft as necessary.

Student self-assessment sheet

HAVING READ THE INTERVIEWS

What I know now about the craft of poetry that I did not know before

---

HAVING DONE THE CREATIVE WRITING TASKS

What I know now about the poets that I did not know before

Ways in which I think my writing has improved

Ways into writing poetry which I can now use that I didn't know before

What I think I could now do better, or move on to in the future

---

HAVING DONE THE READING AND DISCUSSION TASKS

What I now know about the ways in which poets work

What I know now about what to look for as I read, to see how poems are talking to me beyond merely telling me what happens or describing things.

What I would like to read next

HAVING THOUGHT ABOUT ALL THE ACTIVITIES AND INTERVIEWS

My interest in and knowledge of poets and poetry has:

Increased a lot ☐

Increased a little ☐

Not increased ☐

Actually grown less ☐ Tick the box which applies

Poems for Comparative Assignment

(see page 101).

'When I saw you last, Rose'

When I saw you last, Rose,
You were only so high:-
How fast the time goes!
Like a bud ere it blows,
You just peeped at the sky,
when I saw you last, Rose!

Now your petals unclose,
Now your May-time is nigh:
How fast the time goes!

And a life, – how it grows!
You were scarcely so shy,
when I saw you last, Rose!

In your bosom it shows
Thee's a guest on the sly;
(How fast the time goes!)

Is it Cupid? Who knows!
Yet you used not to sigh,
When I saw you last, Rose;
How fast the time goes!

Austin Dobson

The Puzzled Game-Birds

They are not those who used to feed us
When we were young – they cannot be –
These shapes who now bereave and bleed us?
They are not those who used to feed us,
For did we then cry they would heed us.
– If hearts can have such treachery
They are not those who used to feed us
When we were young – they cannot be!

Thomas Hardy

Weary with toil, I haste me to my bed,
The dear repose for limbs with travel tired;
But then begins a journey in my head
To work my mind, when body's work's expir'd:
For then my thoughts – from far where I abide –
Intend a zealous pilgrimage to thee,
And keep my dropping eyelids open wide,
Looking on darkness which the blind do see:
Save that my soul's imaginary sight
Presents thy shadow to my sightless view,
Which, like a jewel hung in ghastly night,
Makes black night beauteous and her old face new.
  Lo! thus, by day my limbs, by night my mind,
  For thee, and for myself no quiet find.

William Shakespeare

It is a beauteous evening, calm and free,
The holy time is quiet as a Nun
Breathless with adoration; the broad sun
Is sinking down in its tranquillity;
The gentleness of heaven brooks o'er the Sea;
Listen! the mighty Being is awake,
And doth with his eternal motion make
A sound like thunder – everlastingly.
Dear Child! dear Girl! that walkest with me here,
If thou appear untouched by solemn thought,
Thy nature is not therefore less divine:
Thou liest in Abraham's bosom all the year;
And worshipp'st at the Temple's inner shrine,
God being with thee when we know it not.

William Wordsworth

Introductory Assignment

The Poet's Language

One thing all the poets agree on is the importance of the words they use. Much of the time we hardly bother to think of the words we use; they are so familiar to us that to have to pause and think of a new one can be a disconcerting experience because usually we don't have to struggle to find ordinary words which will do for most of the encounters we have. If we do have to look for a new word, it is often because we want to express an extra meaning. But meaning is not the only property of words (there are those who would say that meaning is not even a property of words). Poets want particular words for a whole range of uses beyond those needed in everyday speech or writing – even when the appearance and sound of the poem seems to be that of ordinary speech or writing. Poets use the sound of a word; its music in combination with other words; its powers of rhyme, of alliteration, of assonance. Before we look at the assignments based on the poets who have been interviewed, here is some work to do which is designed to lead towards that feeling for the properties and powers of words which all the poets share.

The *Word tree* was developed by Jan Mark (interviewed in *Living Writers 1: Novelists)* and Mick Gowar. It has often been used by them in schools in sessions done as visiting writers. Theoretically, once started it needn't finish until every word in the dictionary has been used. You may find yourselves stopping before that, however.

Word tree

Writers do not have to rely on their own unaided vocabularies. For many writers word lists of their own making, thesauruses and dictionaries of all types are in indispensable aid. The word tree is a way of building your own word list, but based not on the meanings of word (like a thesaurus) nor on alphabetical order (like a standard dictionary), but on the sounds of words. The word tree grows into a stock of words which are linked not only by rhyme (which most people can recognise) but also by assonance and alliteration.

Rhyme is when the endings of two words sound the same – like spin and thin.

Alliteration is when the main consonant sound in a word are the same – brick and break for example.

Assonance is when the vowel sounds of two words are the same – crow and boat.

To start a word tree, write a word at the bottom of a sheet of paper and draw three branches coming from it:

At the end of the left hand branch write a word that rhymes with the word you chose:

At the end of the middle branch write a word which alliterates with the word you started with:

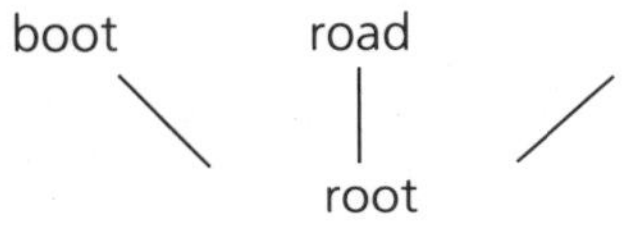

And on the remaining branch write a letter that assonates:

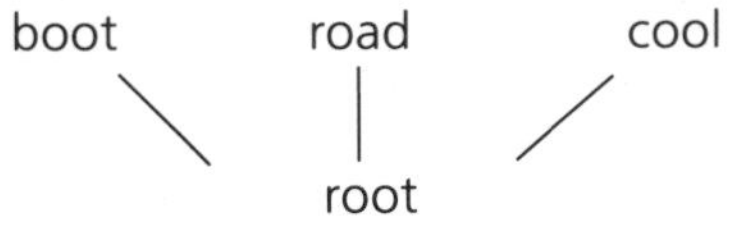

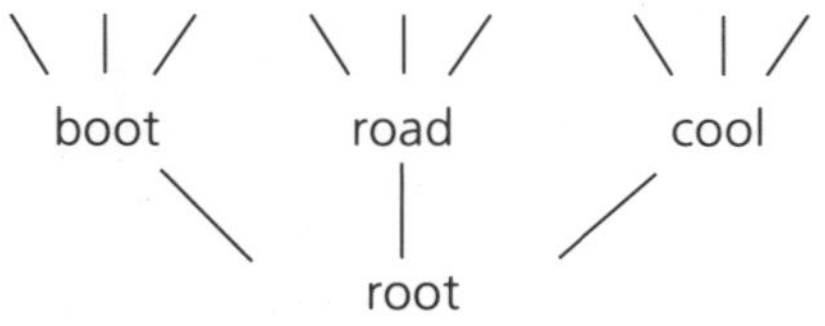

Then for each of your new words draw three branches, and for each write a word that rhymes, alliterates and assonates: then for each of those words three branches … and so on until you have filled the page with words – all linked, through sound, to the word you started with.

You have now completed the first assignment and have something of the raw material of poetry – words and their properties – to take with you on your journey into the thoughts and works of the four poets.

But, as was said at the start of the assignment, it needn't finish until the entire word stock of the language is exhausted. There is no reason why you should not continue your word trees – either on your own or in groups – until they are like Yggdrasil, the tree of the world in Norse mythology, whose roots and branches bound together earth, heaven and hell. Which, after all, is very similar to what language does anyway.

I interviewed Roger McGough on a summer afternoon in the front garden of the house in London where he lives with his wife and two small children. Roger was born in Liverpool, and studied at Hull University where his writing was encouraged by the poet, Philip Larkin, who was the university's librarian.

Roger's work achieved national recognition with the first publication of *The Mersey Sound* ***(Penguin Poets 10) in the sixties, an anthology which also included the work of Adrian Henri and Brian Patten. He was a member of the pop group Scaffold, whose his records included*** *Thank U Very Much* ***and*** *Lily The Pink* ***(which reached number one).***

Although this interview concentrates on Roger's poetry, he is an extremely versatile writer whose work has included stage plays, TV and film scripts, prose fiction and songs. He is also much in demand as a reader of his own work, and has given numerous performances throughout the UK and abroad.

Interview with ROGER McGOUGH

by Mick Gowar

I didn't write any poems at all when I was at school, but I did enjoy reading poems aloud. When I was still very young, my mother decided I should have elocution lessons – the idea then was that you shouldn't have a thick Liverpool accent, you were supposed to lose it – and the one thing I enjoyed about those lessons was reciting things like Jabberwocky.

I began writing when I went to university. I went to Hull University, and as luck would have it, the warden of my Hall of Residence was Philip Larkin. That was the first time I realised you could be a poet and alive at the same time! Until then I'd thought poetry was just English Literature, and that meant The Past. And although Larkin was a very quiet man, a very private man, he was a sort of living embodiment – a poet, and someone whose work I enjoyed.

When I first started writing, I copied the forms I was reading like the French ballads. But then as I read more, I became aware of other sorts of poems; other ways of setting a poem out. And that's a very exciting part of becoming a poet: experimenting; trying out new things; learning how to use the tools of the trade.

But it wasn't just a question of learning the techniques, although that is important. What it all comes down to, I think, is feeling; I was always dealing with emotion and feeling rather than ideas.

For me, in the early days, it was a pure emotional outburst which I tried to shape and control. But of course, in those first poems I wasn't speaking with my own voice; I was using the ghosts of other voices – Dylan Thomas, and the French poets I was studying. It took me a while to discover my own voice; but when I did, I found that it was very close to the voice I speak with.

I was always put off publishing my poems in the university literary magazine – even though Philip Larkin said I should - because all the poems they printed seemed to be full of Latin quotations. It was as if the poets were moving the furniture of their education into their poems: 'Look at me – I've been to Italy ... Hey, man – I can speak French!'

It was the same with the theatre group: all the men seemed to be tall, and very handsome, and had big booming voices, and I thought: 'I'm not like that, so I can't be an actor; I can't be a poet.' This was before all the Albert Finneys and Tom Courtneys, so there were no role models in those days for people with my sort of upbringing. So it all seemed very strange to me; exciting, but strange.

But despite all that, I had a very strong belief in myself. I began sending poems to magazines like *London Magazine and Encounter*, and I even sent a load of poems off to Penguin – straight to the top! They came back with an encouraging letter, but by then – I was in my early twenties – I thought it was only a matter of time before I was accepted! I don't know why I felt like that, but I did.

I came back to Liverpool and got very

the liverpool scene

RECORDED LIVE ALONG THE MERSEY BEAT

EDITED BY EDWARD LUCIE-S

involved in poetry readings. These were mainly influenced by the American Beat Poets – Ginsberg, Ferlinghetti, Coros – and English poets like Christopher Logue, Mike Horovitz, Adrian Mitchell and Pete Brown. We were trying to do the same sort of thing in Liverpool. That's when I first met Adrian Henri and Brian Patten, and it was through the readings that things really started to take off. A chap called John Willis, who was then editor of the *Times Literary Supplement*, saw a reading and recommended me to his agent. She took all my work, and within a year my first book *Frink And Summer With Monika* – a novel and poems – and the Penguin book *The Mersey Sound* came out.

With the *The Mersey Sound* things took off amazingly: full-page features in the *Daily Mirror*, The *Times*, *The Observer*. It was all part of the fashion for Liverpool, the Beatles, and that's how Penguin marketed it.

But we always felt a bit funny about that. For example, when the hard-back book *The Liverpool Scene* came out it was dedicated to the Beatles. We didn't like that, but we were in a dilemma. We could sense all the excitement, and we could see that it might be a good idea commercially, but we didn't want to be packaged as a group. We were all poets; we were all separate – we just met together. But even today, we're still grouped together. At festivals, for example, people still seem to want a Liverpool Poet.

It was about this time too that Scaffold started. It started because at the same time as writing poems I was also writing scripts and sketches, and people like John Gorman would help read out these dialogues as part of poetry readings. And this caused a lot of interest.

You've got to remember that at this time – the sixties – Liverpool had gone from having no media attention to being the centre of it. Media people had started taking the train up to Liverpool – which they thought was very daring – to look for the New Thing. And someone saw a group of us doing a show, and five of us were auditioned. In the end three of us were picked: Mike McCartney, Paul's brother; John Gorman, who's a very funny comedian; and me as the writer. And we became Scaffold.

But at first we didn't do any songs at all. We started off doing weeks satirical improvisations on the news headlines for a programme called *Gazette*, which was broadcast live in the north. And our stage shows were all satire and poetry – no songs. But then because of Mike's connections, and because Brian Epstein was our manager, we started making records. Nothing happened. So we decided to make one last record, and that was *Thank U Very Much* and it was a hit.

And that changed my life in many ways. The next record we made was *Lily The Pink*, which was number one for a long time, and our audience changed from being students to being Mums, Dads and Kids. And we were always being asked questions for these Fanzine pieces like: 'What's your favourite food? ... What's your favourite colour?' And my hobby was always listed as 'writing poetry'. And I realised: Oh God! What has been my life, everything I am – now people think I just write poetry for a hobby!

Scaffold finally broke up around '72 or '73, and we formed Grimms with some of the Bonzos. That grew and grew until it was almost the last of the Big Bands, it was a huge undertaking. But we did some great shows, really enjoyable.

Although I work mainly on my own

now, I still do joint shows with Brian or Adrian or Peter McCarthy. With Brian, we've known each other so long that there's no jealous hoarding of material. We share poems, split them up into different voices, and when people come to our shows its often impossible for them to tell who's written what.

With Peter McCarthy it's much more satire and sketches, like the early stuff with Scaffold. But again, I find I'm in danger of getting classified as a comedian; something other than a poet. We keep getting booked into comedy weeks and festivals, and I'm having to be careful not to get drawn back into being an 'entertainer' again.

I wrote *The Identification* just after the Abercorn bombing. The Abercorn was a restaurant in Belfast which was bombed, and a lot of children were killed and injured. I saw a television interview with the father of one of the boys who had been killed, and he was talking about the experience of identifying his son. I was very moved by it, but I really don't know why I decided to write a poem about it. What I mean is, I see things all the time which move me, but that doesn't necessarily mean I want to write about them. But the strange thing was that much later I saw an unpublished poem by Robert Lowell in his notebooks about the same identification: a father talking about identifying his son, and how he knows it's his son because he has some trick matches in his pocket. Now, I hadn't seen Lowell's poem and he hadn't seen mine, but we'd both been moved to write about exactly the same event.

The Identification took a long time to write, and I had no idea when I started the poem that it was going to end with the discovery of the cigarettes, even though that would seem to be the pivotal point of the poem. In the same way, when I started writing *Hearts and Flowers* I didn't know that it would end with the holy pictures falling out of the missal. In both cases, I didn't have the endings in my mind at all, they came through working through the poem.

Poems like *The Identification* and *Hearts and Flowers* take a long time to write. *Hearts and Flowers* took three or four months, and I wrote nothing else during that time. With both of those poems I was writing and re-writing them because I didn't know where I was going; what was going to happen. But with a poem like *Grobianus* I knew quite early on – almost as soon as I got the idea.– what it was going to be like when it was finished. I'd been reading a book of saints, and discovered that there was a saint of coarse people. All the words – like quibberdicks and quakebuttocks – are all real words which used to be in regular use. Some of them I knew already, others I had to find out. It was great fun to write.

I've written a number of poems about my family: my aunt who used to cover the furniture with blankets because she was mentally ill; *Snipers* about my uncle; and of course *Hearts and Flowers* about Aunt Madge. *Tramp, Tramp, Tramp* is about my grandfather, but the Tramp of the title not only refers to him marching off but also to Charlie Chaplin.

When I knew him, my grandfather was mentally ill – talking to himself, and in a very sad state. And when you see someone like that, you often assume that they've always been like that. But my mother and grandmother were always saying things like: 'It's a pity you didn't know him when he was younger. He was a marvellous man, always very careful what

Roger McGough

he looked like. He was handsome,' they used to say, 'just like Charlie Chaplin.'

He was also a very staunch Catholic. But then at the end of his life, when he was taken to a hospice for the dying, it was as if he was suddenly possessed by the Devil. He began using language he'd never used in his life; he was cursing the nuns who ran the hospice, hitting them. And that's how he died. And my grandmother said, it was almost as if he'd spent all his life preparing for a happy death and at the very last minute he'd blown the whole thing.

Ironically, my Dad used to think we were the only proper ones, the only normal ones, and all the neighbours were bonkers. That's what *Barzydown* means. We were surrounded by these busybody women and he was always saying: 'She's barzydown' – meaning, 'she's round the bend.' And I think it must be a North Liverpool expression, because even a lot of Liverpudlians have never heard it. And what I worked out it meant was, literally: 'His bars are down'; in other words, 'He's got out of the asylum!'

There was also that special kind of working-class pride; always trying to be a little bit better than your neighbours, keeping your front step cleaner than anyone else in the road. Its the sort of thing Willy Russell was talking about when he said that if he writes for anybody, he writes for that kind of working-class family that wants to 'better themselves.' Not the hooligans, but the people who want to get on, read proper books, join the library.

I don't think live readings can take the place of books, but it's often been seeing and hearing people reading their own work which has brought their work alive for me. So that's what I try to do in my own readings. I don't just pick up a book, open it at page one and read straight through it like a talking book. I always see it as a performance, and I take a lot of care choosing which poems I'll read, what order to put them in, and that keeps it fluid for me. I'd hate to get to the stage where I'd be reading poems and not really thinking about what I was doing. I know that's what happens with actors, because it's happened to me with Scaffold or doing comedy. You can be on stage acting your heart out, but all the time you're thinking about whether to have a curry or a doner kebab after the show.

But poetry's different because I'm more involved, and there's always new material to be brought in which keeps it fresh.

I think readings are important because it puts you in contact with your audience. Sometimes, you're writing away and you wonder: 'Who's going to buy this book; is anybody going to read it at all?' But actually writing a poem is still the most exciting thing for me, and readings will never replace that.

Publications

Gig, Cape, 1973.
After The Merrymaking, Cape, 1974.
In The Glassroom, Cape, 1976.
Holiday On Death Row, Cape, 1979.
You Tell Me (with Michael Rosen), Puffin, 1979.
Counting By Numbers, Viking Kestrel, 1980.
Waving At Trains, Cape, 1982.
Sky In The Pie, Puffin, 1983.
Mersey Sound, Penguin, 1983 (with Brian Patten, Adrian Henri).
Second Volume, Penguin, 1983 (with Brian Patten, Adrian Henri).
Editor Strictly Private, Viking Kestrel, 1985.
Melting Into The Foreground, Penguin, 1987.
Selected Poems, Cape, 1989.
Nailing The Shadow, Puffin, 1989.
Imaginary Menagerie, Puffin, 1990.
Pillow Talk, Viking Kestrel, 1990.
Summer With Monika, Penguin, 1990.

Literary terms

Haiku This is a verse form of three lines which originated in Japan. The first line has five syllables, the second seven syllables, the third five again. Haikus are carefully constructed pieces containing a wealth of meaning in a small number of words.

Limerick A short form of comic verse with five lines, usually rhyming aabba. The origin of the limerick form is not known, but it was popularised by Edward Lear in the 19th century.

French ballade A form of medieval French lyric poetry consisting of three stanzas and a final address. Each stanza has the same rhyme scheme and a final line which acts as a refrain.

American Beat Poets The Beat movement was a literary and social movement in 1950's America. It rebelled against conventional society, seeking personal freedom through art, drugs, sex and new ideas. The main centres were the artistic communities of New York, San Francisco and Los Angeles. Prominent writers of the movement included William Burroughs and Allen Ginsberg.

Satire Satire is literary work which ridicules human or social pretensions. It was used by poets as early as Roman times (e.g. Horace). The tradition was continued by poets such as Dryden, Pope and Byron, but in the twentieth century satirists – e.g. Evelyn Waugh – have tended to use prose. Private Eye is a good example of topical political satire.

Assignment 1

First Stage

There are several major points which Roger McGough makes which lead to the distinctiveness of his poems and which we are going to concentrate on.

They are:

- that some may take months to write and how they are going to end isn't clear for a very long time;
- that many of his poems deal with his family (and two of them, *Tramp, Tramp, Tramp* and *Hearts and Flowers*, took a long time to write);
- that the ones which take a long time end with a 'clinching detail', like the cigarettes in *Identification* which brings the whole poem together;
- that readings are important because 'it's often been seeing and hearing people read their own work which has brought their work alive for me' and 'it puts you in touch with your audience' (Roger McGough is probably better known to many people as a performer than as a poet).

The work on these assignments is going to look at these points: first by merely examining some poems, then by moving to some writing and performance of our own.

Second Stage

Here are two poems Roger McGough emphasised a lot; they took a long time to write; in them he reflects on his own experience and tries to account for the people in his family.

Tramp Tramp Tramp

Insanity left him when he needed it most.
Forty years at Bryan & May, and a scroll
To prove it. Gold lettering, and a likeness
Of the Founder. Grandad's name writ small:
'William McGarry, faithful employee'.
A spent match by the time I knew him.
Choking on fish bones, talking to himself,
And walking round the block with a yardbrush
Over his shoulder. 'What for, Gran?' 'Hush ...
Poor man, thinks he's marching off to war.

'Spitting image of Charlie, was your Grandad,
And taller too.' She'd sigh. 'Best-looking
Man in Seaforth. And straight-backed?
Why, he'd walk down Bridge Road
As if he had a coat-hanger in his suit.'

St Joseph's Hospice for the Dying, in Kirkdale,
Is where Chaplin made his last movie.
He played Grandad, and gave a fine performance
Of a man raging against God, and cursing
Nuns and nurses who tried to hold him down.

Insanity left him when he needed it most.
The pillow taken from his face
At the moment of going under. Screaming
And fighting to regain the years denied,
His heart gave out, his mind gave in, he died.

The final scene brings tears to everybody's eyes.
In the parlour, among suppurating candles
And severed flowers, I see him smiling
Like I'd never seen him smile before.
Coat-hanger at his back. Marching off to war.

Hearts and Flowers

Aunty Marge,
Spinster of the parish, never had a boyfriend.
Never courted, never kissed.
A jerrybuilt dentist and a smashed jaw
Saw to that.
To her,
Life was a storm in a holy-water font
Across which she breezed
With all the grace and charm
Of a giraffe learning to windsurf.

But sweating
In the convent laundry, she would iron
Amices, albs and surplices
With such tenderness and care
You'd think priests were still inside.

Deep down,
She would like to have been a nun
And talked of missing her vocation
As if it were the last bus home:
'It passed me by when I was looking the other way.'

'Besides,'
She'd say, 'What Order would have me?
The Little Daughters of the Woodbine?
The Holy Whist Sisters? A glance at the ceiling.
'He's not that hard up.'

We'd laugh
And protest, knowing in our hearts that He wasn't.
But for the face she would have been out there,
Married, five kids, another on the way.
Celibacy a gift unearned, unasked for.

But though
A goose among grown-ups,
Let loose among kids
She was an exploding fireworks factory,
A runaway pantomime horse.

Everybody's
Favourite aunt. A cuddly toy adult
That sang loud and out of tune.
That dropped, knocked over and bumped into things,
That got ticked off just like us.

Next to
A game of cards she liked babysitting best.
Once parents were out of the way
It was every child for itself. In charge,
Aunt Marge, renegade toddler-in-chief.

Falling
Asleep over pontoon, my sister and I,
Red-eyed, would beg to be taken to bed.
'Just one more game of snap,' she'd plead,
And magic two toffees from behind an ear.

Then suddenly
Whooshed upstairs in the time it takes
To open the front door. Leaving us to possum,
She'd tiptoe down with the fortnightly fib:
'Still fast asleep, not a murmur all night. Little angels.'

But angels
Unangelic, grew up and flew away. And fallen,
Looked for brighter toys. Each Christmas sent a card
With kisses, and wondered how she coped alone.
Up there in a council flat. No phone.

Her death
Was as quick as it was clumsy. Neighbours
Found the body, not us. Sitting there for days
Stiff in Sunday best. Coat half-buttoned, hat askew.
On her way to Mass. Late as usual.

Her rosary
Had snapped with the pain, the decades spilling,
Black beads trailing. The crucifix still
Clenched in her fist. Middle finger broken.
Branded into dead flesh, the sign of the cross.

From the missal
In her lap, holy pictures, like playing cards,
Lay scattered. Five were face-up:
A full House of Sacred Hearts and Little Flowers.
Aunty Marge, lucky in cards.

In his interview, Roger McGough talks a lot about the relatives these poems are about. His family means a lot to him.

In your groups, read these poems carefully. Read them silently, read them aloud to each other, all the way through or taking one verse each, until you know how the poems sound as well as knowing what they say.

When you are satisfied that you are not going to get any more out of these poems, discuss what you have read, having regard to these points:

- Does Roger McGough think his family are
  a lot of nutters
  deeply pathetic people
  wonderful people struggling against odds and worthy of remembrance?
- Are these people so individual – even weird – that they can't mean anything to other people except to have a good laugh at their oddness?
- Why should Roger McGough want to expose his family (and himself, by association) in this way?

I don't know what you would have said about the first question, but I think I see bits of all three in Roger McGough's attitude. We are used to portrayals of the 'Liverpool Character' (look at the cast of Bread) and in some ways these poems are in that tradition. But there is a lot more as well because (like all poets) Roger McGough isn't just writing about his immediate subject.

I think that, about the second topic, I would look at *Tramp, Tramp, Tramp* and remember a lot of other poems about the First World War. This is as much a First World War poem as Wilfred Owen's are. Think what life at home afterwards would be like for such of the soldiers Owen wrote about who might have come back. And it is also a grim view of how we die alone which applies to everyone. We don't know how we are going to die – but poems like this rehearse possible ways for us. 'There but for the grace of God go I'. It is important that literature is there to do this for us.

In the third, I think I would see a special poignancy about why he writes like this. There is a big clue in his interview, when he talks about why he didn't act at university:

'This was before all the Albert Finneys and the Tom Courtneys so there were no role models in those days for people with my sort of upbringing.'

Roger McGough's generation was the first for whom being an actor or poet (or top politician or captain of industry for that matter) was possible for everyone and not just those from a particular social class. Conversely, then, proper life-chances were not open to his family; they are trapped in their place, their time, their class, their broken bodies, and this, to Roger McGough, is tragic. And – as for so many – only the luck of being born at a particular time saved him from the same fate which had he suffered it he would not be able to express. Now he can do it for them.

Third Stage

We are not going to try to write poems like these. We are going to think – about people we know, family or friends, of a different generation from ours; their lives and possibly their deaths. Note down a few ideas – description, narrative, memory – about them, but don't at this stage attempt to turn these into a poem.

Something you think or write may stick; this may be the start of a long writing process for you. You may recall other assignments in previous books in this series – the 'photograph' assignment in the work on Adèle Geras's interview, for example. However, perhaps nothing will stick at all – it may, like many ideas which come to writers, lead nowhere. There may be no significance in it, so don't worry if it leads nowhere – or goes underground for weeks, months, years and then reappears as something worth writing about.

2

First Stage

Here is Roger McGough's poem *The Identification*

The Identification

So you think it's Stephen?
Then I'd best make sure;
be on the safe side as it were.
Ah, there's been a mistake.
You see, it's black, now Stephen's fair ...
What's that? The explosion?
Of course, burnt black. Silly of me.
I should have known. Then let's get on.

The face, is that a face I ask?
That mask of charred wood
blistered, scarred, could
that have been a child's face?
The sweater, where intact, looks
in fact all too familiar.
But one must be sure.

The scoutbelt. Yes that's his.
I recognised the studs he hammered in
not a week ago. At the age
when boys get clothes-conscious
now you know. It's almost
certainly Stephen. But one must
be sure. Remove all trace of doubt.
Pull out every splinter of hope.

Pockets. Empty the pockets.
Handkerchief? Could be any schoolboy's.
Dirty enough. Cigarettes?
Oh this can't be Stephen.
I don't allow him to smoke, you see.
He wouldn't disobey me. Not his father.

But that's his penknife. That's his all right.
And that's his key on the keyring
Gran gave him just the other night.
So this must be him.
I think I know what happened
... about the cigarettes.
No doubt he was minding them
for one of the older boys.
Yes, that's it.
That's him.
That's our Stephen.

Roger McGough

In your groups read it – as before, silently and then aloud to each other.

Notice what he says about this: 'I had no idea when I started the poem that it was going to end with the discovery of the cigarettes.'

Now, in your groups, re-read *Hearts and Flowers*. Look at the end again. Then see what Roger Mcgough says about that: 'In the same way when I started writing *Hearts and Flowers* I didn't know that it would end with the holy pictures falling out of the missal. In both cases I didn't have the endings at all; they came through working through the poem.'

There is nothing more to do in these assignments other than read and talk about these poems, take to heart what Roger McGough says and then understand these truths about writing, which all the writers in this series would assert:

- that the only way to know what you want to write is to write it;
- so meticulous planning and structuring beforehand in stories and poems often doesn't work because you are unfolding a structure, not building it. Writing lets the subconscious mind work.

3

First Stage

Roger McGough writes in other ways as well. He writes quickly and humourously and he performs. He mentions one poem in particular which came quickly – *St Grobianus*. Here it is.

Prayer to Saint Grobianus:
The patron saint of coarse people

Intercede for us dear saint we beseech
    thee
We fuzzdutties and cullions
Dunderwhelps and trollybags
Lobcocks and loobies.

On our behalf seek divine forgiveness for
We puzzlepates and pigsconces
Ninnyhammers and humgruffins
Gossoons and clapperdudgeons.

Have pity on we poor wretched sinners
We blatherskites and lopdoodles
Lickspiggots and clinchpoops
Quibberdicks and Quakebuttocks.

Free us from the sorrows of this world
And grant eternal happiness in the next
We snollygosters and gundyguts
Gongoozlers and groutheads
Ploots, quoobs, lurds and swillbellies.

As it was in the beginning, is now, and
    ever shall be,
World without end. OK?

St Grobianus is 'the patron saint of coarse people'. Roger McGough is not afraid to be coarse. Here is another of his quick, humourous – and coarse – poems:

Bottom

Who'd be a bottom? Not me.

Always facing the wrong way.
To go for a walk
And not be able to see
Where you are going.

To be sat upon all day.
Smacked. Called rude names.
Whistled at. Laughed at.
The butt of a hundred jokes.

Faithful to the end.
An undercover agent
Working all hours
And getting no thanks for it.

Alas, poor bottom.

This is a very clever little poem; the bottom is seen as a character with a separate existence, a mind and feelings of its own. The last line looks back to Shakespeare's Hamlet – 'Alas poor Yorick'.

In your groups, read these poems aloud to each other, trying out different sorts of delivery. I think you will find it confirmed that they are funny poems and that they come to life even more when performed.

Second Stage

In your groups, think about a communal performance poem based on the body. Assign a part of the body to each group member (within reason – you must have some regard for what is going to be suitable for public performance). Then each person should attempt a short poem in any form you want about that part – doing what Roger McGough does; seeing it as a separate character with a life of its own.

You can use free verse, rhyme, limerick. You may take a clue from another 'body part' poem – the insistent *This is the house that Jack Built* rhythm of Michael Rosen's *This is the hand* (to be found in *Mind Your Own Business,* Deutsch 1974).

Third Stage

Now arrange a group 'body poem' performance to the whole class, where you can declaim to them all.

When this is done, you might find yourself with a whole 'head to toe' communal body poem, perhaps with some parts covered twice with interestingly different characteristics. It might be worth displaying or desk-top publishing the final epic result.

Roger McGough

4

First Stage

One of the forms listed in the Literary Terms (page 27) is the haiku. This is a small verse form of 5-7-5 syllables per line which originated in Japan. It is very likely that you have written in this form yourself in previous years. Here is a trick haiku by Roger McGough.

First Haiku of Spring

cuck oo cuck oo cuck
oo cuck oo cuck oo cuck oo
cuck oo cuck oo cuck

This is a true haiku because its syllables are exactly 5-7-5. And yet it's not, because the reason haikus work so well is that they are little highly-wrought moulds you can pour lots of meaning into and that doesn't happen in this haiku because it is just playing around and says nothing.

Or does it? Does this playing around with forms and words give a meaning beyond that of words in a particular order?

In your groups discuss whether this haiku is anything more than a game.

You might remember:

- that there is often great competition in newspapers to record the hearing of the first cuckoo in spring and the composer Frederick Delius wrote a wonderful piece of music called *On hearing the first cuckoo in spring*.
- At both the start and end of spring the cuckoo's call seems to be a bit wonky and irregular; it takes some time to warm up – like spring itself.

The poem may be an essay in expressing the waywardness of the cuckoo's call at the start of spring before it really gets going; this may in some way stand for the difficulties of putting meaning into poetic forms like the haiku until they really get going.

But it may not; the poem may be meant as no more than doodle.

DISCUSSION

In your groups, discuss this question:

- If you believe that the poem has a meaning along the lines of what I wrote above and you put this to Roger McGough and he said 'Rubbish', would that mean that the meaning isn't there and you would have no right to believe it is?

If you can come up with a convincing answer to this question you will have performed a miracle, because the question of whether literature has meaning beyond what the author intended has exercised people's minds since literature began.

Second Stage

The haiku is a very pointed form. Here is a whole series of them: a complete poem by another contemporary poet, Anthony Thwaite.

A Haiku Yearbook

Snow in January
Looking for ledges
To hide in unmelted.

February evening:
A cold puddle of petrol
Makes its own rainbow.

Wind in March:
No leaves left
For its stiff summons.

April sunlight:
Even the livid bricks
Muted a little.

Wasp in May
Storing his venom
For a long summer.

Morning in June:
On the sea's horizon
A white island, alone.

July evening:
Sour reek of beer
Warm by the river.

August morning:
A squirrel leaps and
Only one branch moves.

September chestnuts:
Falling too early,
Split white before birth.

October garden:
At the top of the tree
A thrush stabs an apple.

November morning:
A whiff of cordite
Caught in the leaf mould

Sun in December:
In his box of straw
The tortoise wakes.

Anthony Thwaite

Here is another 'calendar poem', this time by Roger McGough – *A Cautionary Calendar*.

A Cautionary Calendar

Beware January,
His greeting is a grey chill.
Dark stranger. First in at the kill.
Get out while you can.

Roger McGough

Beware February,
Jolly snowman. But beneath the snow
A grinning skeleton, a scarecrow.
Don't be drawn into that web.

Beware March,
Mad Piper in a many-coloured coat
Who will play a jig then rip your throat.
If you leave home, don't go far.

Beware April,
Who sucks eggs and tramples nests.
From the wind that molests
There is no escape.

Beware May,
Darling scalpel, gall and wormwood.
Scented blossom hides the smell
Of blood. Keep away.

Beware June,
Black lipstick, bruise-coloured rouge,
Sirensong and subterfuge.
The wide-eyed crazed hypnotic moon.

Beware July,
Its juices overflow. Lover of excess
Overripe in flyblown dress.
Insatiable and cruel.

Beware August,
The finger that will scorch and blind
Also beckons. The only place you will find
to cool off is the morgue.

Beware September,
Who speaks softly with honeyed breath.
You promise fruitfulness. But death
Is the only gift that she'll accept.

Beware October,
Whose scythe is keenest. The old crone
Makes the earth tremble and moan.
She's mean and won't be mocked.

Beware November,
Whose teeth are sharpened on cemetery stones,
Who will trip you up and crunch your bones.
Iron fist in iron glove.

Beware December,
False beard that hides a sneer.
Child-hater. In what year
Will we know peace?

Anthony Thwaite's poem takes little scenes and associations for each month – they read like personal associations – and puts them in haiku form. Roger McGough's poem is also a regular form, this time rhyming, but its tone is grim; every month is seen as a harbinger of death.

DISCUSSION

- This is a perfectly reasonable way of looking at the months of the year. Does the fact that he wrote it thus mean that this is the only way Roger McGough sees them?

Well, I myself would doubt this very much. One thing Roger McGough and his poetry should have left us in no doubt about is how many and various are the moods poetry can take and how many uses it can be put to. These 'calendar poems' stand as a good example.

Third Stage

In Assignment 2 you each chose a different part of the body for a communal poem. Now you should each agree on a month of the year, so you have one to write about towards a 'communal calendar' poem of your own.

For this you must agree on:

whether you will all use the same form (e.g. the haiku)

whether you will all adopt the same tone (e.g. will it be grim like Roger McGough's, reflective like Anthony Thwaites's or ironically amusing like *January brings the snow* by Flanders and Swann?)

Fourth Stage

The final 'calendar poem', like the body poem, should be performed and published.

Like her creation, the poet Jason Strugnell (whose deliberately appalling and very funny verses were published in *Making Cocoa for Kingsley Amis*)***, Wendy Cope lives in South London. But there the similarity ends. Whereas Strugnell's flat would, like the man himself, be a sordid mess, the flat where I spoke to Wendy was neat, orderly and attractive.***

Wendy was born in 1945. After studying History at St Hilda's College, Oxford, she taught in primary schools in London for fifteen years.
She worked as Arts and Reviews Editor for Contact, the ILEA newspaper for teachers, from 1982 to 1984, and was the TV critic for The Spectator. She is now a freelance writer.
In addition to writing poetry for adults, Wendy has also published a book of original finger rhymes for young children, and edited a selection of poems by women poets for teenage readers.

Interview with WENDY COPE

by Mick Gowar

I didn't really start writing poems until I was twenty-seven, although I did go through a phase when I was about thirteen when I wrote some really ghastly poems. I remember there was one about Princess Margaret's wedding, and one about a pop singer I was very much in love with at the time – I'm not going to tell you which one.

I didn't think about writing poems at all when I was in my mid and late teens, but I did enjoy reading poetry – particularly Keats – and I remember thinking that the best thing that could possibly happen would be to marry a great poet like Keats, and be his 'soulmate', and live in a garret with him. I didn't envisage a 'soulmate' having to do any housework, and it certainly didn't occur to me that I could write poetry. I think a lot of women get muddled up like that between what they want to be and what they want to marry.

I studied History at university, and although I'd occasionally read a book of poetry I mostly forgot about it until I became a primary school teacher and started doing some creative work with the children. That was what helped me to discover the creative side of myself. I found that when I had an idea for a creative writing lesson, I would have in my head a very clear idea of the poem I wanted the children to write. Also, I found that when a child wrote a poem I felt that I knew exactly what needed to be done to make the poem better (although I didn't necessarily tell them).

Gradually, I discovered that I enjoyed writing poems myself, but I didn't know whether I had talent or not. I went on a lot of courses – especially Arvon courses – and I joined a weekly evening class which was run by Blake Morrison. I read a lot and experimented a lot, but it was a long time before anyone wanted to publish any of my poems.

I particularly enjoyed the Arvon courses because it felt so wonderful to be with people who were all interested in poetry. If you become interested in poetry when you're at university you can join the college Poetry Society, and there are probably lots of people around who are interested too. But if you're already working – as I was – it can be very difficult to find anyone to talk with; you can get very isolated. So the Arvon courses were very stimulating because they gave me the chance to test out things I'd discovered against other people's experiences, and simply to be with people, all day every day, who were as interested in poetry as I was.

I stopped going on courses when I was published in a Faber *Poetry Introduction* – because it would have been embarrassing – but I still miss them, and I'd certainly recommend them to others. I didn't write much when I was actually there, but I found I wrote a lot when I got back: they got me going. I still find that prolonged contact with other poets – at poetry festivals, for example – can be stimulating in the same way.

There are two main ways that tutors

can help students on writing courses. The first is criticism, when you look at a poem someone has written and say what you like or don't like about it, and how it can be improved. The other is stimulus; actually getting people going because there may be people who have never written before, or people who are stuck with working on a folder of old poems and what they really need is to start something new.

When I'm running courses I try and give people time to just write, but I also like to have sessions when everyone's together and we play various games. For example, giving people ten minutes to write a poem; or putting pictures in envelopes and each person has to write about the picture they get. One thing I have done, which was my own idea and worked very well, was to put in each envelope a piece of paper with two simple words on like 'I was' or 'And then.' The only rule was that each person's poem had to begin with the two words they got. And also games like *The Exquisite Corpse*, which is like Consequences. The first person writes an article on a piece of paper, then folds it and passes it on to the next person who writes down an adjective, then they pass it on to the next who writes a noun ... and so on. That game was played by the Surrealists and the first time they played it they got the sentence: 'The exquisite corpse murdered the blue poem.'

I really enjoy playing those games, and occasionally quite good poems come out of playing them.

I knew that *Making Cocoa For Kingsley Amis* was a book which had a large potential audience, I was sure that if people knew about the book they would buy it because I'd been doing quite a lot of readings and I knew that people enjoyed the

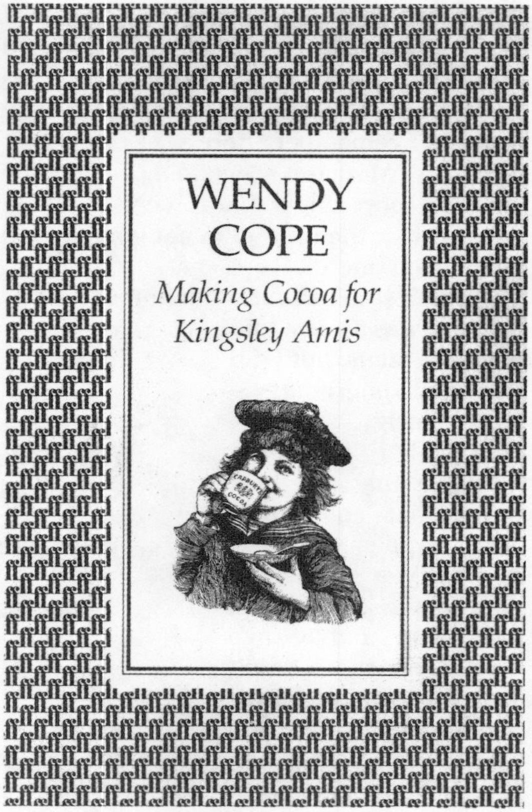

poems. I really wanted to break through to the sort of audience which a lot of my friends are part of: people who are reasonably well-educated and literate, and who buy novels but wouldn't normally think of buying a book of poems. But the publicity the book got was more than I expected, and it was really too much for me because I didn't have an agent or anybody to advise me. Here I was, living in a grotty little flat in South London and suddenly all these journalists and photographers were descending on me; people were ringing up all the time asking me to appear on television. It was really as if I was being asked to do 25 terrifying things before breakfast every day.

But the good thing about all that publicity was that it did help the book to sell and brought offers of freelance work. I was able to give up my teaching job and start to earn my living as a freelance writer.

I wrote *Tich Miller* one August. It was the school holidays, so I was determined to write something while I had some time to myself. But when you try to write like that an awful thing often happens: you sit down at your desk, in front of a blank sheet of paper, and you can't think of a thing to write about. So I decided to free-associate. I just put my finger on the page of any old book and I got a word; and I'd write down that word and anything that came into my head just to see what happened.

Doing this, I found that I was starting to think about my childhood, and I was writing down all sorts of memories about my childhood. And I suddenly started thinking about this girl, and I realised that this was something I wanted to write a poem about.

Once that had happened the poem itself came very quickly, and when I'd finished it I took it to a workshop group I was part of at the time. But they were very iffy about it. They didn't like the ending – in fact for a long time nobody else liked the ending of *Tich Miller* – but I refused to change it. Sometimes what other people say is right; their advice echoes your own doubts. But I knew that was how I wanted the poem to end.

But I had another worry with that poem because it was based on a real person, and she did die. And I thought: what if her family read it and find it upsetting? So I changed her name, and I also found that other details changed. For example, I wasn't called Tubby at primary school – that was later; and the age at which she died was different. So it was interesting to me to see how bits of fiction crept in, but I don't think it really falsified the poem.

I do believe that poetry is about telling the truth – it's especially important not to

put on an act about your own feelings – but poets are allowed to write fiction too. Fiction is fiction, but if it's true to life, and it's true to the way people are, then in a way it is true even if the writer made it all up.

One of the things I like about using traditional forms and metres is that there are rules to guide you, but you still need to have a feeling for it. I'm not an expert on scansion; I know a bit, but I think it's more important to read and to use your ears. If I've got any doubts about a form, I'll read to see what other people have done. If I was writing a sonnet, for example, I'd read Shakespeare – see what he does, what he gets away with – and work out from that how much you can bend the rules.

Peter Redgrove says somewhere: 'A poem has to find its own form.' Quite often my poems will start off in one form – say a triclet – and then I'll realise that the form is wrong, it's not long enough. Rondeau redoublé went through a stage of being a villanelle until I decided it needed to be longer. But I didn't know what else there was, so I got out a reference book and had a look for another form to try. So I tried it as a rondeau redoublé and – which is what usually happens when I try a new form for the first time – I got it wrong and had to start again.

I think my musical training was very useful to me when I started to write in strict forms because in musical theory the rules are much stricter than poetry; you have to get things exactly right. Also, having a feeling for music must help you develop a feeling for music in poetry, including rhythm.

When people are trying to explain what poetry is, they often say that one of the special qualities of poetry – whether it's in a strict form or in free verse – is rhythm. But now that I'm writing more prose, it seems to me that getting the rhythm right is just as important in prose as in poetry. Of course, with prose and free verse there aren't as many rules to guide you. And I must admit that I've always been the kind of person who looks for rules – I often find them helpful. Though I'm keen on the old rules – about how to write a sonnet or a limerick – and enjoy following them, I'm aware of another set of rules – the unwritten ones that say what kind of thing we're allowed to write nowadays. It's important to understand those too, and then break them as often as possible.

Publications

Making Cocoa For Kingsley Amis, Faber, 1986.
Twiddling Your Thumbs, (Hand-rhymes for under-7s), Faber, 1988.
Editor: *Is That The New Moon*, Lions Teen Tracks, 1989.
River Girl (Ill. Nicholas Garland), Faber, 1991.
Across The City, Priapus ~Booklet.
Poems From A Colour Chart of House Paints, Priapus Booklet.
Men And Their Boring Arguments, Priapus Booklet.

Literary terms

Traditional forms and metres The rules of metre, rhyme and stanza form are often called prosody, and as Wendy Cope points out they are very similar in a number of ways to the rules of music. She mentions 'scansion' which is the metrical scanning of the verse. Metre is the formal and regular organisation of rhythm, and the names of the different metres – iambic, trochaic, etc. – are like the time signatures in music – 3/4, 4/4; waltz time, march time. And just as music is divided into separate bars which are the basic repeating units of rhythm, so a line of verse can be divided into feet or normally two or three syllables. The most off-putting thing about prosody for most people is that the names of the different metres are Greek. But remember, the basic language of cooking is French, and most musical terms are Italian. if you do get familiar with the language of prosody, the terms will soon seem no more threatening than 'piano', 'cello', 'sauté' or 'braise'.

Here is a little memory aid to help with metre. It was written by the Romantic poet Coleridge for his sons Hartley and Derwent. When they were schoolboys they had difficulty learning which metre was which, so he wrote them this mnemonic:

From: *Metrical Feet* by Samuel Taylor Coleridge

Trochee trips from long to short;
From long to long in solemn sort
Slow Spondee stalks; strong foot: yet ill able
Ever to come up with Dactyl trisyllable.
Iambics march from short to long; –
With a leap and a bound the swift Anapaests throng;
One syllable long, with one short at each side
Amphibrachys hastes with a stately stride; –
First and last being long, middle short, Amphimacer
Strikes his thundering hoofs like a proud high-bred racer.

Villanelle This form is thought to have originated in Italy in the late 1400s. The name means 'rural song', although modern villanelles deal with a wide variety of subjects. Only two end rhymes are allowed and the first and third lines must be repeated according to a strict pattern throughout the poem. There are six stanzas in all: five stanzas of three lines each and a final stanza of four lines. An example of a villanelle is *First Love* by Mick Gowar. See also page 103.

Triolet This is the smallest of the French stanzaic poems. Like the villanelle, the rhyme scheme is restricted to two end rhymes and whole lines are also repeated. It is eight lines long, and the rhyme scheme is: ABaAbAB.

An excellent example of a triolet is Thomas Hardy's *The Puzzled Game-Birds* see page 17.

Sonnet This is the most widely known and widely used stanza form in English. There are two main traditional sonnet forms, one of one stanza and one of two. Both types of sonnet have a total of fourteen lines, and the metre is iambic pentameter in both.

The English or Shakespearean sonnet is the single stanza form. It has a rhyme scheme ababcdcdefefgg. Although a single stanza, the English sonnet consists of four distinct sections: three *quatrains*, or groups of four lines, and a final *couplet*. Traditionally the English sonnet has been used to present an argument or dilemma with the first quatrain putting one point of view, the second a different or contradictory point of view, the third proposing a compromise or resolution to the conflict and the couplet providing a summing-up or conclusion.

The Italian or Petrachan sonnet again has fourteen lines, but divided into two stanzas; the first of eight lines, but divided into two stanzas; the first of eight lines (known as the *octet*) and the second of six lines (*sestet*). The rhyme scheme of the octet is invariable abbaabba, but the sestet can rhyme in a number of ways, the commonest being either cdcdcd or cdecde. Like the English sonnet, the Italian sonnet has often been used to express differing points of view of one experience, or contrasting or changing feelings.

Because the sonnet is a comparatively popular form, examples are easily found. For the English sonnet, the best examples are of course Shakespeare's own sonnets. A fine example of the Petrachan or Italian sonnet is Keats's *On First Looking Into Chapman's Homer*. Tony Harrison, the contemporary British poet has written excellent sonnets in both forms.

Rondeaux redoublé A rondeau is a short lyrical poem using an intricate verse form developed in fourteenth and fifteenth century France. Rondeaux were usually ten or thirteen lines long, using only two rhymes, and had an elaborate repetitive pattern of words and lines.

Surrealism This was a revolutionary movement across all the arts which demanded complete freedom for the imagination from all the old conventions of morality, reason, logic and good taste. The basic belief of the surrealists was that true knowledge could only be found in the unconscious mind (which expressed itself through dream, hallucinations and visions) and that this unconscious should be the source of all art. Surrealism is generally associated with the recreation of dreams, nightmares and hallucinations; the dislocation of time and logic; the apparently random mixing up of unconnected and often weird and shocking images. Although very few writers can be described as 'pure' surrealists, this general style has been very widely used and extremely influential.

Examples of surrealist art include the paintings of Rene Magritte and Salvador Dali.

Rene Magritte: Le Reproduction Interdite 1937

Assignment 1

Wendy Cope says a lot in her interview about getting the right form for a poem. She likes the fact that there are rules to guide you which have been found to work by other poets and she says, 'If I've got any doubts about a form, I'll read to see what other people have done'. This is very similar to what Aidan Chambers says in his interview in *Living Writers 1: Novelists* – '... I'd discovered by accident how you become a writer: by copying.'

At first, neither of these statements sound very impressive: however, if we think about them in three separate ways, they become very important.

(i) Only by working through and trying out for ourselves what other people have tried to do can we find our individual voices.

(ii) Alexander Pope, a poet of the eighteenth century, said in his *Essay on Criticism*:

True wit is Nature to advantage dress'd;

What oft was thought, but ne'er so well express'd.

(iii) The poet and critic T S Eliot, in an important essay called *Tradition and the Individual Talent*, said that whether we like it or not, we are all part of a great tradition stretching back for centuries. Whatever we write is part of it – even if we are rebelling against it. So whenever something new is written and read, the relationship of all other works changes slightly, both to each other and to the new work.

Here are four drafts and the final version of a poem by Wendy Cope called *Rondeau Redoublé*. In it, she is saying something of importance to herself and, she feels, to all women. But the problem of guessing right in our friendships and human relationships applies as much to men as to women and there is a sort of bitter-sweet recognition of truth in the poem for many readers.

In your groups, look carefully at these successive drafts. Read them silently, read them aloud to each other, get to know them as well as you can.

Rondeau Redoublé

There are so many kinds of awful men –
One can't avoid them all. She often said
She'd never make the same mistake again:
She always made a new mistake instead.

The chinless type who made her feel ill-bred;
The practised charmer, less than charming when
He talked about the wife and kids and fled –
There are so many kinds of awful men.

There are so many kinds of ~~hopeless~~ awful men –
One can't avoid them all. She often said
She'd never make the same mistake again:
She always made a ~~different one~~ new mistake instead.

The chinless type who made her feel ill-bred;
The half-crazed hippy, deeply into Zen,
Whose cryptic homilies she came to dread –
There are so many kinds of ~~hopeless~~ awful men.

The practised charmer, less than charming when
He talked about the wife and kids and fled;
The drunk who fell asleep at nine or ten –
The ~~One can't avoid them all~~, she often said.
overfed

The ageing banker, rich and overfed
Who talked about the dollar and the yen –
Though there were many more mistakes ahead,
She'd never make the same mistake again.

The solemn budding poet, scribbling in his den
Odes not to her but to his ~~cat now dead~~ pussy fed;
The fervent youth who worshipped Tony Benn –
She always made a new mistake instead.

And so the gambler was at least unwed
And didn't preach or sneer or wield a pen
Or ~~[illegible]~~ or take the scalpel to bed –
She lived and learned and lived and learned but then

There are so many kinds.

Or hoard his ~~dough~~ wealth

~~Long odes to his~~
~~bland poetry, fed~~

Wendy Cope

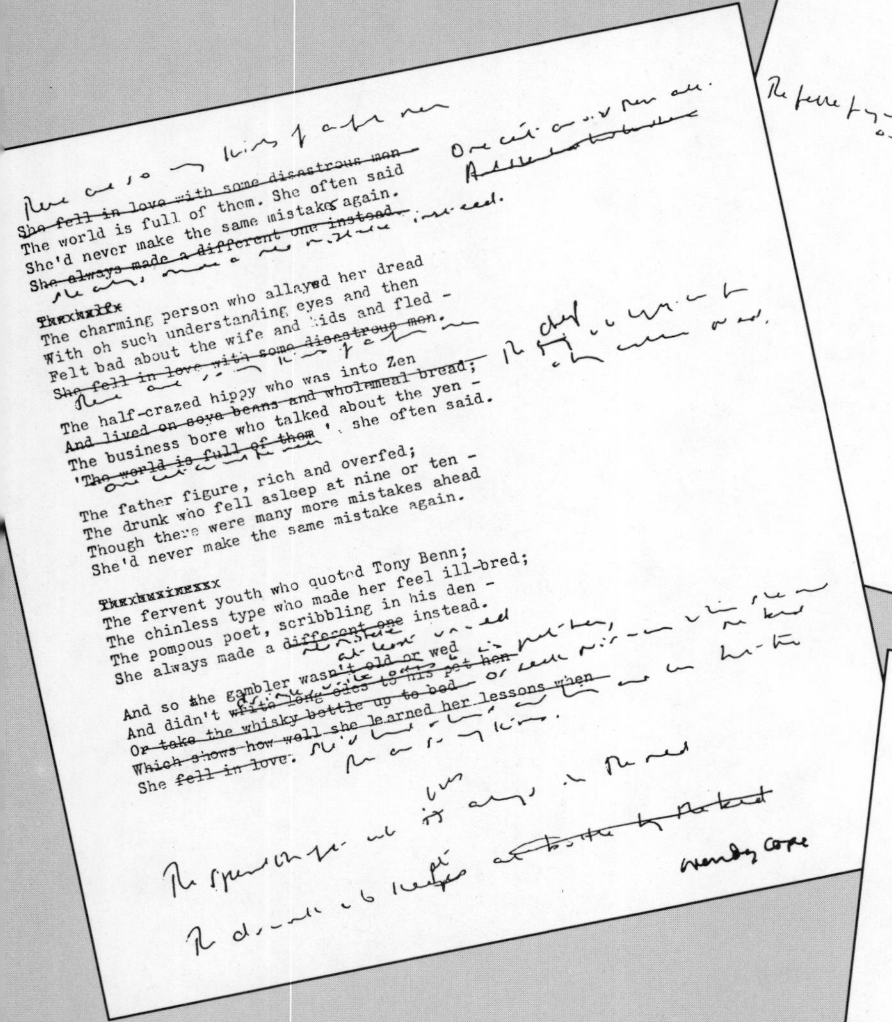
She fell in love with some disastrous men
The world is full of them. She often said
She'd never make the same mistakes again.
She always made a different one instead.

Thexxxxx
The charming person who allayed her dread
With oh such understanding eyes and then
Felt bad about the wife and kids and fled -
She fell in love with some disastrous men.

The half-crazed hippy who was into Zen
And lived on soya beans and wholemeal bread;
The business bore who talked about the yen -
'The world is full of them', she often said.

The father figure, rich and overfed;
The drunk who fell asleep at nine or ten -
Though there were many more mistakes ahead
She'd never make the same mistake again.

Thexxxxxxxx
The fervent youth who quoted Tony Benn;
The chinless type who made her feel ill-bred;
The pompous poet, scribbling in his den -
She always made a different one instead.

And so the gambler wasn't old or wed
And didn't write long odes to his pet hen
Or take the whisky bottle up to bed -
Which shows how well she learned her lessons when
She fell in love.

Wendy Cope

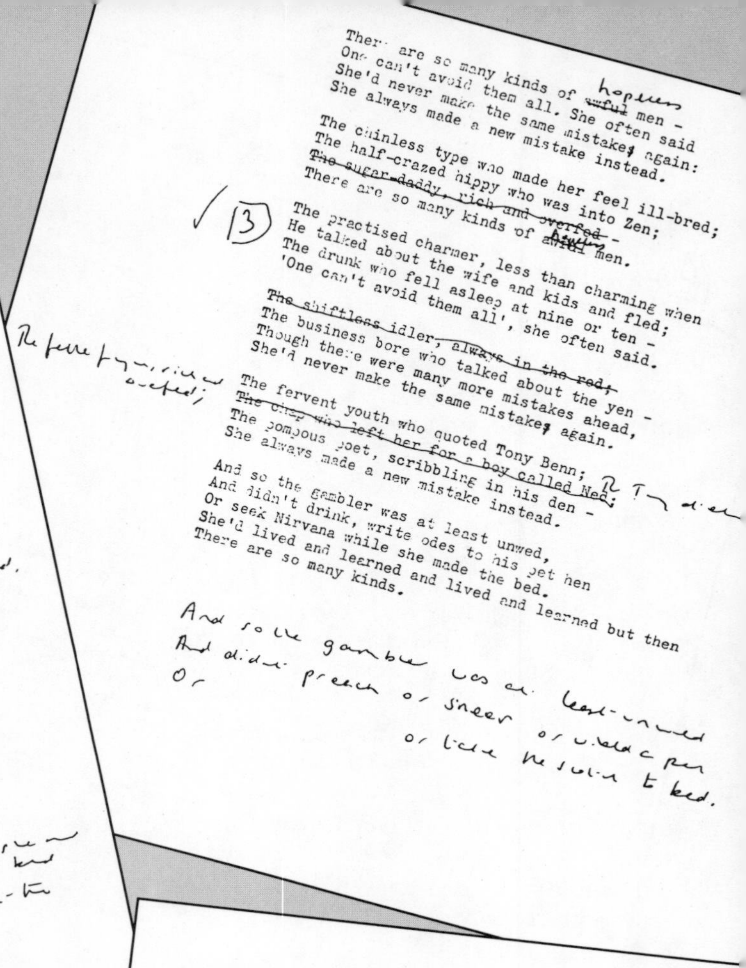
There are so many kinds of awful men - hopeless
One can't avoid them all. She often said
She'd never make the same mistake; again:
She always made a new mistake instead.

The chinless type who made her feel ill-bred;
The half-crazed hippy who was into Zen;
The sugar-daddy, rich and overfed -
There are so many kinds of awful men.

The practised charmer, less than charming when
He talked about the wife and kids and fled;
The drunk who fell asleep at nine or ten -
'One can't avoid them all', she often said.

The shiftless idler, always in the red;
The business bore who talked about the yen -
Though there were many more mistakes ahead,
She'd never make the same mistake; again.

The fervent youth who quoted Tony Benn;
The chap who left her for a boy called Ned;
The pompous poet, scribbling in his den -
She always made a new mistake instead.

And so the gambler was at least unwed,
And didn't drink, write odes to his pet hen
Or seek Nirvana while she made the bed.
She'd lived and learned and lived and learned but then
There are so many kinds.

And so the gambler was at least unwed
And didn't preach or sneer or wield a pen
Or take the sherry to bed.

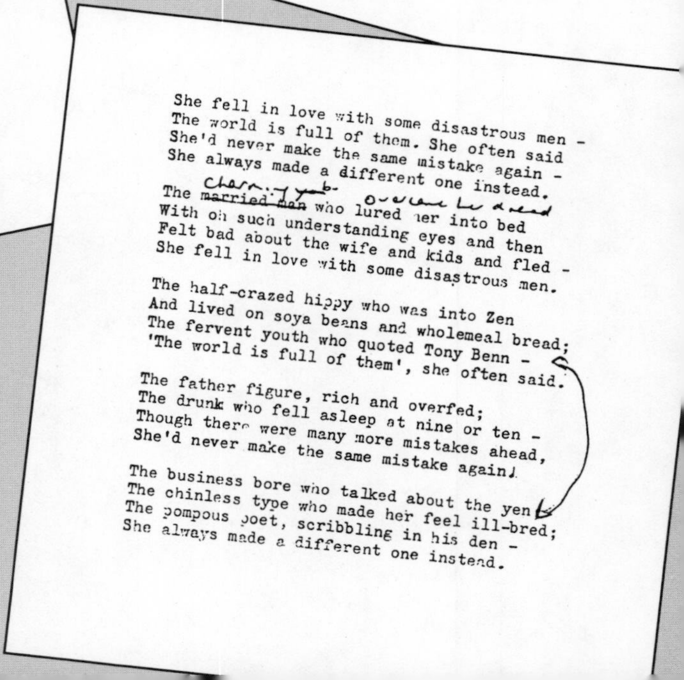
She fell in love with some disastrous men -
The world is full of them. She often said
She'd never make the same mistake again -
She always made a different one instead.

Charming
The married man who lured her into bed
With oh such understanding eyes and then
Felt bad about the wife and kids and fled -
She fell in love with some disastrous men.

The half-crazed hippy who was into Zen
And lived on soya beans and wholemeal bread;
The fervent youth who quoted Tony Benn -
'The world is full of them', she often said.

The father figure, rich and overfed;
The drunk who fell asleep at nine or ten -
Though there were many more mistakes ahead,
She'd never make the same mistake again.

The business bore who talked about the yen
The chinless type who made her feel ill-bred;
The pompous poet, scribbling in his den -
She always made a different one instead.

The half-crazed hippy, deeply into Zen,
Whose cryptic homilies she came to dread;
The fervent youth who worshipped Tony Benn –
'One can't avoid them all,' she often said.

The ageing banker, rich and overfed,
Who held forth on the dollar and the yen –
Though there were many more mistakes ahead,
She'd never make the same mistake again.

The budding poet, scribbling in his den
Odes not to her but to his pussy, Fred;
The drunk who fell asleep at nine or ten –
She always made a new mistake instead.

And so the gambler was at least unwed
And didn't preach or sneer or wield a pen
Or hoard his wealth or take the Scotch to bed.
She'd lived and learned and lived and learned but then
There are so many kinds.

DISCUSSION

(i) How does the poem change? Is the final version significantly better than the first?

(ii) Is the final version as good as it could possibly be?

(iii) What is the main reason for her successive changes?

I don't know what any of your answers would have been – but I would have found great difficulty in giving final answers to any of them. Most of the changes are for the placing of lines and rhymes; the poem's thought is hardly affected. Wendy Cope could have spent months tinkering with the poem; if she ever republishes it in a collected edition of her work she may well want to make some alteration. The truth is, as the French poet and critic Paul Valéry said, a piece of writing is never finished; it is only at some point abandoned.

2

First Stage

Many of Wendy Cope's poems deliberately refer to other poets. In her book *Making Cocoa for Kingsley Amis* there are two nursery rhymes – 'baa-baa black sheep' as it might be written by William Wordsworth and 'Hickory-dickory dock' as if by T S Eliot. There is also *My Lover*, which is a clear reworking of the eighteenth century poet Christopher Smart's wonderful poem *For I will consider my cat Jeoffry*. Wendy Cope's versions are witty and say a lot about the original poets. In *My Lover* she writes a funny, affectionate and moving poem which can stand by itself but which gains much more from knowing Christopher Smart's poem.

For I Will Consider my Cat Jeoffry

For I will consider my cat Jeoffry.
For he is the servant of the Living God duly and daily serving him.
For at the first glance of the glory of God in the East he worships in his way.
For this is done by wreathing his body seven times round with elegant quickness.
For if he meets another cat he will kiss her in kindness.
For one mouse in seven escapes by his dallying.
For he counteracts the powers of darkness by his electrical skin and glaring eyes.
For he is an instrument for the children to learn benevolence on.
For the English Cats are the best in Europe.
For he knows that God is his Saviour.
For there is nothing sweeter than his peace when at rest.
For he is of the Lord's poor and so indeed is he called by benevolence
perpetually – Poor Jeoffry! Poor Jeoffry! the rat has bit thy throat.
For I bless the name of the Lord Jesus that Jeoffry is better.
For by stroking him I have found out electricity.
For he can tread to all the measures upon the musick.

Christopher Smart

My Lover

Wendy Cope

For I will consider my lover, who shall remain nameless.
For at the age of 49 he can make the noise of five different kinds of lorry changing gear on a hill.
For he sometimes does this on the stairs at his place of work.
For he is embarrassed when people overhear him.
For he can also imitate at least three different kinds of train.
For these include the London tube train, the steam engine, and the Southern Rail electric.
For he supports Tottenham Hotspur with joyful and unswerving devotion.
For he abhors Arsenal, whose supporters are uncivilized and rough.
For he explains that Spurs are magic, whereas Arsenal are boring and defensive.
For I knew nothing of this six months ago, nor did I want to.
For now it all enchants me.
For this he performs in ten degrees.
For first he presents himself as a nice, serious, liberated person.
For secondly he sits through many lunches, discussing life and love and never mentioning football.
For thirdly he is careful not to reveal how much he dislikes losing an argument.
For fourthly he talks about the women in his past, acknowledging that some of it must have been his fault.
For fifthly he is so obviously reasonable that you are inclined to doubt this.
For sixthly he invites himself round for a drink one evening.
For seventhly you consume two bottles of wine between you.
For eighthly he stays the night.
For ninthly you cannot wait to see him again.
For tenthly he does not get in touch for several days.
For having achieved his object he turns again to his other interests.
For he will not miss his evening class or his choir practice for a woman.
For he is out nearly all the time.
For you cannot even get him on the telephone.
For he is the kind of man who has been driving women round the bend for generations.
For, sad to say, this thought does not bring you to your senses.

* * *

For he inspires poem after poem.
For he is clean and tidy but not too concerned with his appearance.
For he lets the barber cut his hair too short and goes round looking like a convict for a fortnight.
For when I ask if this necklace is all right he replies, 'Yes, if no means looking at three others.'
For he was shocked when younger teammates began using talcum powder in the changing-room.
For his old-fashioned masculinity is the cause of continual merriment on my part.
For this puzzles him.

- In your groups, read *For I will consider my cat Jeoffrey* and *My Lover* to each other. You will need to know that when Christopher Smart wrote *Jeoffrey* he was regarded as mad and shut away in Bedlam. Does this make any difference to the way you understand it?
  You might also like to know that *Jeoffrey* is part of a much longer poem Smart wrote called *Jubilate Agno* (*Rejoice in the*

Lamb). There are two opposed sections in it, one answering the other. In one section the lines begin with 'Let …'; in the other, with 'For …'

DISCUSSION

- Does knowing *Jeoffrey* add to the effect of *My Lover*?
- Do you think the lover would be very pleased at being written about in the same terms as a lunatic's cat?
- Does this mean Wendy Cope sees her lover as a figure of fun? Is he therefore devalued?

I don't know what you would have said but I think that, though *My Lover* does gain from knowledge of *Jeoffrey* (it becomes a sort of poetical joke) it stands on its own without it. The feeling I get from it is one of an amused affection: the lover becomes an interesting, unique – and lovable – character in his own right as well as being merely a lover. You might look at *Living Writers 2: Dramatists* and the idea of the 'inimitable' character dealt with in the assignment on Phil Redmond.

I also get from *Jeoffrey* a feeling of the great love Christopher Smart had for his cat – at the time his only friend and companion. For Wendy Cope to refer to her lover in these terms – having regard to that same quality of uniqueness and inimitability Jeoffrey transmits – far from demeaning him, raises him to a very high place indeed.

Second Stage

These poems are written in a form which is lovely to use. Take something or someone – friend, relative, pet – or object – recalcitrant car, motor-bike, football team – and try writing a 'For I will consider …' poem on her/him/it/them.

Then share/perform/print/publish your poems.

3

First Stage

Now we are going to look at a reworking of a far more familiar sort of text.

In your groups, read this poem by Wendy Cope.

Reading Scheme

Here is Peter. Here is Jane. They like fun.
Jane has a big doll. Peter has a ball.
Look, Jane, look! Look at the dog! See him run!
Here is Mummy. She has baked a bun.
Here is the milkman. He has come to call.
Here is Peter. Here is Jane. They like fun.

Go Peter! Go Jane! Come, milkman, come!
The milkman likes Mummy. She likes them all.
Look, Jane, look! Look at the dog! See him run!

Here are the curtains. They shut out the sun.
Let us peep! On tiptoe Jane! You are small!

Here is Peter. Here is Jane. They like fun.

I hear a car, Jane. The milkman looks
glum.
Here is Daddy in his car. Daddy is tall.
Look, Jane, look! Look at the dog! See
him run!

Daddy looks very cross. Has he a gun?
Up milkman! Up milkman! Over the wall!
Here is Peter. Here is Jane. They like fun.
Look, Jane, look! Look at the dog! See
him run!

DISCUSSION

- What does this poem remind you of?
- What is the story she is telling?
- What makes the poem – always provided that you think it *is* – funny?

I don't know what you would have said but I would have identified the Primary School reading scheme book (*Janet and John* or *Ladybird*, perhaps). I would have extracted a story about adultery which is sad and funny at the same time – funny for the situation itself, which reminds me of old Max Miller jokes, seaside postcards and Benny Hill sketches; sad in real life for all the people involved, especially the children. I might have said that the humour comes from the collision of the two elements – the serious implications of the adult story and the child's eye view of the world the 'reading scheme' language portrays. If pressed to explain this further I might point out how the words 'fun' and 'likes' take on far greater width of meaning here from what they would have in a real Reading Scheme book.

Second Stage

Here is a simple writing exercise. Look again at the poem and then compare it with a page from an actual Reading Scheme book. Remember that most Reading Schemes are written to enable children to *recognise* words, not necessarily to *understand* them. As pieces of writing they are about as different from poetry as it is possible to be.

Then, singly, in pairs or small groups, do what Wendy Cope did; write a 'grown-up' story in the convention of a reading scheme.

Note: Wendy Cope uses reading scheme vocabulary but she also uses strict metre and form. you may find it more suitable at first simply to use the scheme format and only go on the rhythm, rhyme and metre if you feel able to.

4

First Stage

Here is another of Wendy Cope's poems.

Waste Land Limericks

I
In April one seldom feels cheerful
Dry stones, sun and dust make me fearful;
Clairvoyantes distress me,
Commuters depress me –
Met Stetson and gave him an earful.
II
She sat on a might fine chair,
Sparks flew as she tidied her hair;
She asks many questions,
I make few suggestions –
Bad as Albert and Lilt – what a pair!
III
The Thames runs, bones rattle, rats creep;
Tiresias fancies a peep –
A typist is laid,
A record is played –
Wei la la. After this it gets deep.
IV
A Phoenician called Phlebas forgot
About birds and his business – the lot,
Which is no surprise,
Since he'd met his demise
And been left in the ocean to rot.
V
No water. Dry rocks and dry throats,
Then thunder, a shower of quotes
From the Sanskrit and Dante.
Da. Damyata. Shantih.
I hope you'll make sense of the notes.

When you have read these poems, your reaction may be – 'So what? They mean nothing. Limericks surely should have real points to them and not need explanation.'

True. You need to know that the five limericks stand together and retell/paraphrase/ respond to/poke fun at (whatever verb you like) TS Eliot's great poem *The Waste Land*.

You may then say, 'Why did we not then read *The Waste Land* first so we could know what all the limericks were about?'

There are several reasons. One is *The Waste Land* is very long and extremely difficult. Another is that just because Wendy cope wrote these after TS Eliot wrote *The Waste Land* it doesn't mean they have to be read after. They can equally well serve as an introduction. By writing these limericks, Wendy Cope is proving the point T S Eliot himself makes that was mentioned earlier, about everyone being in a tradition and therefore dependent on each other.

Second Stage

DISCUSSION

With the piece of information about tradition in mind but without looking at *The Waste Land*, consider in your groups why Wendy Cope wrote *Waste Land Limericks*.

You might consider the reasons below and you might come up with some more.

- She thinks *The Waste Land* is an awful load of pompous nonsense and wants to make fun of it, to deflate it.
- She, on the other hand, thinks it is wonderful and wants to pay homage to it.
- She was stuck for a subject and simply copied Eliot.
- She wrote it to enable people to come to *The Waste Land* for the first time with

some idea of what it was all about, having read her limericks first.

- She wrote it so people who knew *The Waste Land* might find more enjoyment in it as well as appreciating her limericks.
- She wrote it so she herself could begin to make more sense of *The Waste Land*.

Perhaps there was something of all those reasons in Wendy Cope's decision to write *Waste Land Limericks*.

The Waste Land is in five sections, each of a different length. Each limerick refers exactly to one section and compresses its content into limerick form. To do this sort of thing, you need to have read the original very carefully and understand it well. So both writer and reader are helped to understand better the original – the writer by getting the limerick accurate and pointed; the reader by referring the limerick back to the original.

Third Stage

Here is a poem written in 1818 by the Romantic poet Percy Bysshe Shelley:

Ozymandias

I met a traveller from an antique land
Who said: Two vast and trunkless legs of stone
Stand in the desert ... Near them, on the sand,
Half sunk, a shattered visage lies, whose frown,
And wrinkled lip, and sneer of cold command,
Tell that its sculptor well those passions read
Which yet survive, stamped on those lifeless things,
The hand that mocked them, and the heart that fed:
And on the pedestal these words appear:
'My name is Ozymandias, king of kings:
Look on my works, ye Mighty, and despair!'
Nothing beside remains. Round the decay
Of that colossal wreck, boundless and bare
The lone and level sands stretch far away.

Here is a limerick (not by Wendy Cope) based on it:

A man in the desert alone
Found two ginormous legs made of stone
By a great king long dead.
'Give up now,' the man read
On the ruins, and heard the wind moan.

This may not be perfect, but it tries to recapture something of the poet's point. The last line isn't there just to make the rhyme; it also attempts to underline the lonely desolation of the scene which is important to the meaning of the original poem.

Now take some other poems which you know. See if you can write limericks based on them; we may have *The Daffodils Limerick*; the *On first looking into Chapman's Homer Limerick*, even the *Strange Meeting Limerick*.

Don't, by the way, feel that it is wrong to turn poems regarded by the whole world as great, serious and moving into such trivial-seeming things as limericks. If a poem, or any other work of art, is good enough, it can stand any amount of rough handling and emerge with much more understanding and respect from the handler.

Fourth Stage

Now share your limericks with the group and with the whole class. This should be a celebration.

Fifth Stage

Now go back to the poem you chose and attempt an account – you can either write this down or simply tell the others in your group – of what you now know about that poem you chose that you didn't know before as a result of trying to turn it into a limerick.

5

First Stage

Wendy Cope doesn't only write poems which refer to the work of other poets. Some of her poems have no such basis as that at all. Notice how much space in her interview Wendy Cope gives to her poem *Tich Miller*.

Tich Miller wore glasses
with elastoplast-pink frames
and had one foot three sizes larger than the other.

When they picked teams for outdoor games
she and I were always the last two
left standing by the wire-mesh fence.

We avoided one another's eyes,
stooping, perhaps, to re-tie a shoelace,
or affecting interest in the flight

of some fortunate bird, and pretended
not to hear the urgent conference:
'Have Tubby!' 'No, no, have Tich!'

Usually they chose me, the lesser dud,
and she lolloped, unselected,
to the back of the other team.

At eleven we went to different schools.
In time I learned to get my own back,
sneering at hockey-players who couldn't spell.

Tich died when she was twelve.

This is a simple, moving account of the past with a sting in the tail. The episode and the character of *Tich Miller* plainly mean much to Wendy Cope.

But look carefully at her account of how the idea came into her mind, how it changed from being a reminiscence of actuality into a piece of fiction with the altering of certain details and yet stayed true. Wendy Cope says, 'Fiction is fiction, but if it's true to life, and it's true to the way people are, then in a way it is true, even if the writer made it all up.' Here, she is saying something which is central to all narrative, whether in novel, play or poem.

Second Stage

In your groups, read *Tich Miller* carefully.

DISCUSSION

There is more to this poem than simply sadness at the hopelessness and early death of Tich. Wendy Cope seems to be saying something else: there is an edge to her sadness which is more than mere sympathy. What is it? How far is the poem about:

- Tich Miller?
- people generally (in the shape, here, of the rest of the teams)?
- Wendy Cope herself?

Were you struck by the poem's irony? When little, the two stood together and were equal, jeered at and rejected by their peers. But life allowed the poet to 'sneer' at her former tormentors and go on to success. For Tich Miller, though, things would always be like that until her early death. Wendy Cope feels the irony in this. So it's about all three, fairly equally.

Third Stage

You've now had a close encounter with this poem and the process which led to its being written. In your groups, reminisce to each other about events in the past which may be seen to have the same sort of significance and resonance as this one that Wendy Cope chose, so may be worth writing about in this way.

Then, singly, in pairs or in your group, see if you can take one episode – or join two or three episodes together – into an account on the lines of *Tich Miller*.

You may find the episodes don't fit with what you want to say about them. No matter: look again at what Wendy Cope says about the first part of the writing process for *Tich Miller*. Don't be afraid, in your account, to write about what *ought* to have happened if it is more suitable than what *did*.

Tich Miller is a comparative rarity in Wendy Cope's poetry in that it does not rhyme. Would it have lost effect if it had rhymed?

But see how regular the three-lined stanzas are and how effective the single line at the end becomes in comparison.

Try to cast your own account into an unobtrusive free-verse form akin to that of *Tich Miller*.

It would be unfair to describe Craig Raine simply as 'a poet', because his career to date has also included teaching English Literature at university, literary journalism and criticism and magazine and book publishing. At the time I interviewed him, Craig was working as Poetry Editor at the publishing house of Faber and Faber – a post which the newspapers never tired of pointing out had once been occupied by T S Eliot. Since the interview, Craig has taken up a new job, teaching at Oxford University.

Craig was born in County Durham in 1944, and was educated at Oxford University. He has been editor of *Quarto* ***magazine, Books Editor of*** *The New Review* ***and Poetry Editor of*** *The New Statesman.*

As well as writing poetry, Craig has also written the libretto of an opera *The Electrification Of The Soviet Union* ***and has published a collection of his literary essays.***

Interview with CRAIG RAINE

by Mick Gowar

I started writing poetry when I was about sixteen. I was in the Sixth Form, and it seemed to be a clever thing to do – like wearing a bow tie. I wrote a couple of poems which must have been pretty nonsensical and sent them to Philip Toynbee at *The Observer*, who wrote back a very sweet letter saying that I should learn about rhyme and metre.

I also showed them to my English master. We pretended that they were by a friend of mine – a convenient fiction – and he said to me: 'Your friend must stop using 'I' in his poems' and 'Your friend must learn about rhyme and metre.'

He also said: 'These poems are like pimply Dylan Thomas!' You see, although he was a great help, he wasn't an enthuser; he didn't praise indiscriminately. He was tremendously critical, and I remember battling with him from the ages of eleven to eighteen because he was always making us be more critical about our work than we wanted to be. And that was actually a very good training.

Another thing he did was to get us interested in contemporary literature – which was rare in those days. (When I took 'A' level the most modern book on the syllabus was *Sons and Lovers*; apart from that it was all Milton and Chaucer.) He had a whole series of cardboard folders in his room which were full of the reviews and criticism of the latest Wesker, the latest Beckett etc. Any articles he could find, any profiles, were there, and we could take these away and read them. It was a marvellous teaching technique, I now think.

I arrived at university with a folder of bad poems and tried to get them published. Very sensibly, all the editors of university magazines saw that they weren't very good and turned them all down.

What I wrote as an undergraduate was prose: bad pastiches of Hemingway. Then I did a post-graduate degree, and I suppose I'd been doing that for about a year when I met a girl I was very keen on. She asked me: 'What do you do?' So I said: 'I'm a post-graduate student.' And she said, 'Yes, but what do you really want to do?' So I said: 'Oh, I'm a poet!' And she said: 'That's marvellous – can I see some of your poetry?' So I had to start writing – very fast! That's perfectly true!

But my first poem wasn't published until 1973 – ten years after I'd first gone to university – when I was 31.

All young poets begin by copying other poets they admire, and I very much admired Ted Hughes and Robert Lowell. So I turned out these Robert Lowell poems and Ted Hughes poems – and I knew they were good, because they were Hughes poems and Lowell poems. What I didn't realise was that they didn't belong to me: they weren't my poems; they weren't in my voice.

Then one day – in my case, when I was about 26 – it just happens that you stop turning out 'reproduction furniture' and you actually design something which is you. And when your friends read it they say: 'Gosh, this is just like you!' And that means you've found your own voice.

But it can take a long time – over four years in my case – when you're writing like yourself, but people don't recognise it. What editors are too often looking for are – say – Hughes poems and Lowell poems which aren't quite as imitative as your early efforts were, but are still recognisable. It makes them feel comfortable; they can see where it comes from. If you have a new voice, people feel very uncomfortable with it; they can't hear it for a long time.

I think there are two main things a young poet has to do. Firstly, as Ezra Pound said: 'Make it new.' The other thing is to learn the craft – which is what my English teacher said to me, and what Philip Toynbee said to me.

It's important to learn the craft, because you can't actually make anything new until you know what's been done already. You have to master the craft in order to change it; to be able to introduce a new tool – like a carpenter who invents a jig-saw. He'll say: 'Look at this! It can cut in and out; do this and that ...' And it's a marvellous invention, but it can't be invented before the saw. Before it can be invented you've got to be able to use a hammer, pincers, pliers and a saw.

So in poetic terms, you need to know about rhyme and metre in order to appreciate what it is to – say – break metre; what kind of effect it will have if you break metre in the middle of a line.

But once you've mastered the craft the obligation is, yes of course, to 'Make it new.' Originality is, I think, a very important element in art. There's no interest in merely repeating what your predecessors have done. It was new to them, but they've done it.

The Butcher is a good example of how I write a poem, and of how many different things go into a poem.

I suppose the starting point is that I like watching butchers. And one of the necessary conditions of being a writer is that you have to have a necessary idleness. That's to say, you need lots of time (when you're not writing, or reading books) to just go out and look at things – 'loafing around' as it looks. And your family don't quite understand why this is a necessary part of the process of writing, but it is. So you stand around, and you watch people very carefully (actually, you are working very hard because you see everything). And you decide that you like the butcher, and you're going to write about the butcher – which is what I did.

Now, the second thing that went into my butcher poem was James Joyce. One of the greatest influences on me was reading Joyce's *Ulysses*; and there's a fantastic passage in that book in which Leopold Bloom, the hero, goes into a butcher's shop and buys a kidney. And this passage is about a page and a half long. And when I read it I thought: 'This man Joyce can make anything interesting'. And I realised then that the narrow prescription of lyric poetry – that you can only write about love, death and madness – is actually misleading; you can write about anything. So part of my butcher poem was written in competition with Joyce. It sounds terrible and conceited, but you have to set your sights high; you have to take on the great writers. So there was an element of competing with Joyce.

I was also very interested in borrowing from the other art forms. It seems to me that one of the ways you can 'Make it new' is to borrow something from a compa-

Pablo Picasso: The Three Musicians.

rable art, and I'd been looking at Picasso's Cubist paintings and wondering: 'What would a Cubist poem look like?' Cubist paintings shift the viewpoint the whole time: you don't have a static viewpoint, and the object or person is seen from many different angles. And I thought: 'What would be the equivalent in poetry of the viewpoint changing?' It would be to mix your metaphors; something you're not supposed to do because it's supposed to be against 'the rules'. Very interesting, therefore, to mix metaphors and see what you come up with. And what you come up with is a coherent poem – it's very difficult to keep coherence out of art, and particularly out of a poem.

So if you look at the ingredients of this one poem, you have: liking butchers and wanting to look at them; being led and loafing around (but also being very careful in how you see things); reading a passage by James Joyce; and thinking about Picasso and Cubism.

Eliot says somewhere that when a poet is working at the top of his form he's receptive to everything – reading Spinoza, the sound of his typewriter, boiling an egg – everything somehow comes together in the poem. What happens is that the poet becomes a kind of focus for disparate experiences.

What happened in the case of *In The Kalahari Desert,* was that my wife had an ancester called Isabella Price who was a missionary; and we've got a pamphlet at home called *Isabella Price*: *Pioneer*, published by the Missionary Society in about 1888. My wife had read this, of course, and she was dead keen that I should read it, and eventually I did.

What happens in the poem is taken from that book – truncated and telescoped – but essentially it's the true story of a group of missionaries who went into the Kalahari Desert and had a disastrous time.

Now, at the same time as reading the pamphlet I happened to be listening to that news programme, *The PM Programme*, and I heard an interview with Arthur Askey. (It must have been his 80th birthday, or something like that because they were broadcasting a short, magazine piece about his life.) He was talking about how he'd been brought up in Liverpool by his aunt and uncle because he was an orphan, and he described this invariable daily routine. Every day the *Liverpool Post* would come through the letterbox around tea-time, and his uncle would sit down and read it aloud while his wife put on the kettle to make tea. And every time he got to a word he didn't understand, or couldn't pronounce he just said: 'Manchester.'

I was intrigued by it. It was so bizarre that I wrote it in my notebook and thought nothing more about it. But when I started writing the poem, these two 'sources' – Arthur Askey and the Missionary Society Pamphlet – sort of docked in inner space; and in the finished poem, Arthur Askey is just as important as the pamphlet. What gives the whole poem meaning is the notion of 'Manchester'; the notion of where you should be.

In *A Martian Sends A Postcard Home* the reader has to decode what's going on from the clues that are given – like a crossword puzzle – but there are rules and there are solutions; and the reader can piece together what's happening from the information given.

And that goes for any poem: there should be rules; there should be solutions. That's to say that poetry should mean something, and the reader should

know that there is a meaning there.

But that's not to say that it should be too easy. For example, when I describe the lavatory as 'a punishment room ...' it's important that, before you realise it's a lavatory, you've had to live with those lines for long enough that, even after you've worked out the solution, you still can't expel whatever sort of odd notion you first had about the 'punishment room.' So that after that the whole idea of the lavatory is very strange; it should leave you with an eerie feeling that won't go away.

All poems mean different things to different people, because they bring different life experiences to bear. For instance, there's a song in my opera *The Electrification Of The Soviet Union* which is a widow's song; a woman lamenting the death of her husband. Whenever I read that in public, there's always at least one widow in the audience who comes up to me afterwards and says 'Thank you very much.' It obviously means more to someone who has actually lost a husband than to somebody who hasn't.

In that sense, meaning is different, but it's the same. Poems are aesthetic machines; and they're arranged by the writer so that there are right interpretations and wrong interpretations. If you write a poem describing an alarm clock and someone says that it's a bomb, it's really quite close. But if they say it's about a filing cabinet then they're miles off; they're just not taking into account what you've put there.

So there is a sense in which all poems mean different things to different people; but at the same time there is a consistent meaning within which the different meanings have their part. 'Whatever I say as a reader ...' isn't good enough. You have to be able to justify what you say against the text. The text is like a kind of maze; if you follow it properly you can only arrive at the centre – if you take long enough.

Publications

The Onion Memory, OUP, 1978.
A Martian Sends A Postcard Home, OUP, 1979.
Rich, Faber, 1984.
The Electrification Of The Soviet Union, Faber, 1986.
Haydn And The Valve Trumpet: Literary Essays, 1990.
A selection of this poetry available on *Faber Poetry Cassette*.

Literary terms

Rhyme, alliteration and assonance Terms used to describe ways in which repeating patterns of sound are created in a poem. *Rhyme* is the most familiar, and is when the endings of words sound the same e.g. complete/feet. *Alliteration* is when consonant sounds are repeated e.g. foul/feet. *Assonance* is when vowel sounds are repeated e.g green/feet.

Rhyme schemes The conventional way to describe a rhyme scheme is by giving each line–ending rhyme a letter of the alphabet, and showing repeating lines as capital letters.

Lyric poetry Craig Raine talks of 'the narrow prescription of lyric poetry' only being about 'love, death and madness'. More widely, lyric poetry expresses the writer's own thoughts and feelings, usually briefly and in stanzas.

Narrative poetry In contrast to lyric poetry, narrative poetry tells a story or presents facts.

Metaphor Metaphor is applying a name or descriptive word or phrase to something to which it is not literally applicable, for example Craig Raine refers to 'coiled necklaces' of mince in his poem *The Butcher* (see page 00). Mixing metaphors is using a combination of inconsistent metaphors.

Cubism A style of painting and sculpture which originated with Picasso and Braque in the early 1900s. Multiple viewpoints of everyday objects results in a complex of geometrical shapes.

Assignment 1

First Stage

We are carrying on the idea of how poets write, how they think and how they see. In his interview, Craig Raine talks particularly of these ideas:

- that by copying others you find out who you are;
- that before you can experiment in any trade, you must learn the basic craft.

These are themes which are constant with all the poets as well as many of the other writers we have dealt with. Craig Raine leads us to a new view of how this might be done:

- you make things new by looking and thinking and skewing things round in your mind and 'borrowing from other art forms', not just other poetry;
- the poet becomes 'a focus for disparate experience' – everything becomes grist to his mill.The first of Craig Raine's poems that we will look at is *The Butcher*.

The Butcher

'And even St George – if Gibbon is correct – wore a top hat once; he was an army contractor and supplied indifferent bacon'

(E M FORSTER, *Abinger Harvest*)

Surrounded by sausages, the butcher stands
smoking a pencil like Isambard Kingdom Brunel ...
He duels with himself and woos his women customers,
offering thin coiled necklaces of mince
heart lamé-ed from the fridge, a leg of
pork like a nasty bouquet, pound notes
printed with blood.
He knows all about nudity – the slap and trickle
of blood, chickens stripped to their aertex vests.
He rips the gauze from dead balletic pigs,
And makes the bacon slicer swish its legs.
How the customers laugh! His striped apron
gets as dirty as the mattress in a brothel ...
At 10, he drinks his tea with the spoon held back,
and the Great Eastern goes straight to the bottom.

- In your groups, read this poem silently, aloud to each other, taking each verse in turn – as many ways as you can until you think you have got as much as possible out of it.
- Now consider in your groups any odd features that you might notice – points

where you might well ask yourself, 'what on earth is the man talking about?' For example:

Why are there two lots of dots?

Why do they seem to be a sort of frame?

Who built the *Great Eastern*?

Why do the verbs move from 'woos' to 'rips'?

Did any of you at first misread 'slap and trickle' as 'slap and tickle'?

Might Craig Raine have meant you to? Why?

What is going on here?

Note what Craig Raine says: that the poem was the result of just 'loafing around' and watching.

Second Stage

This poem, Craig Raine tells us, was also the result of admiring a piece of writing by someone else – James Joyce, the great Irish writer. In *Ulysses*, Leopold Bloom goes to the butcher and buys a kidney.

Here is that passage.

He halted before Dlugacz's window, staring at the hanks of sausages, polonies, black and white. Fifty multiplied by. The figures whitened in his mind unsolved: displeased, he let them fade. The shiny links packed with forcemeat fed his gaze and he breathed in tranquilly the lukewarm breath of cooked spicy pig's blood.

A kidney oozed bloodgouts on the willowpatterned dish: the last. He stood by the nextdoor girl at the counter. Would she buy it too, calling the items from a slip in her hand. Chapped: washing soda. And a pound and a half of Denny's sausages. His eyes rested on her vigorous hips. Woods his name is. Wonder what he does. Wife is oldish. New blood. No followers allowed. Strong pair of arms. Whacking a carpet on the clothesline. She does whack it, by George. The way her crooked skirt swings at each whack.

The ferreteyed porkbutcher folded the sausages he had snipped off with blotchy fingers, sausagepink. Sound meat there like a stallfed heifer.

He took up a page from the pile of cut sheets. The model farm at Kinnereth on the lakeshore of Tiberias. Can become ideal winter sanatorium. Moses Montefoire. I thought he was. Farmhouse, wall round it, blurred cattle cropping. He held the page from him. interesting: read it nearer, the blurred cropping cattle, the page rustling. A young white heifer. Those mornings in the cattlemarket the beasts lowing in their pens, branded sheep, flop and fall of dung, the breeders in hobnailed boots trudging through the litter, slapping a palm on a ripemeated hindquarter, there's a prime one, unpeeled switches in their hands. He held the page aslant patiently, bending his senses and his will, his soft subject gaze at rest. The crooked skirt swinging whack by whack by whack.

The porkbutcher snapped two sheets from the pile, wrapped up her prime sausages and made a red grimace.

– Now my miss, he said.

She tendered a coin, smiling boldly, holding her thick wrist out.

– Thank you, my miss. And one shilling threepence change. For you, please?

Mr Bloom pointed quickly. To catch up and walk behind her if she went slowly, behind her moving hams. Pleasant to see first thing in the morning. Hurry up,

damn it. Make hay while the sun shines. She stood outside the shop in sunlight and sauntered lazily to the right.

He sighed down his nose: they never understand. Sodachapped hands. Crusted toenails too. Brown scapulars in tatters, defending her both ways. The sting of disregard glowed to weak pleasure within his breast. For another: a constable off duty cuddled her in Eccles Lane. They liked them sizeable. Prime sausage. O please, Mr Policeman, I'm lost in the wood.

– Threepence, please.

His hand accepted the moist tender gland and slid it into a side-pocket. Then it fetched up three coins from his trousers' pocket and laid them on the rubber prickles. They lay, were read quickly and quickly slid, disc by disc, into the till.

– Thank you, sir. Another time.

A speck of eager fire from foxeyes thanked him. he withdrew his gaze after an instant. No: better not: another time.

– Good morning, he said, moving away.

– Good morning, sir.

No sign. Gone. What matter?

In your groups, discuss these points:

- What do you notice about this passage?
- What differences are there between the prose and the poem?

The poem is much, much shorter, but what other differences are there?

Well, while both use language in ways which are far from ordinary, there are differences as well as similarities. The Joyce passage is hard to read as a piece of consecutive prose. Because it is so much longer than the poem, does this mean that it wastes words?

Look again at the *Ulysses* passage. There is one big difference. We see through Bloom's eyes and he is as interested in the 'nextdoor girl', wanting to 'catch up and walk behind her if she went slowly, behind her moving hams' as he is in the contents of the butcher's shop. There are ideas here in the narrative which are transferred into the poem in a different way – the uses of the word 'hams' is important here – which make it a poem while the other (even if written poetically) is prose narrative. Think back to how you answered the question I asked earlier – 'What is going on here?'. – and see if that gives a notion of the difference.

- Now look at what Craig Raine says in his interview about Picasso and Cubist painting. Does this give a further clue?
- Look at some paintings by Picasso. Look in particular at his famous *Guernica*, painted as a result of probably the first serious modern mass air raid on a civilian population. This is a good example of how a wealth of association and reference can be gained by skewing the way we see things so that a lot can be said in a short time.

In your groups, read the poem to each other and to yourselves. When you feel you have got all you can out of it, try thinking about some of the ideas Craig Raine has discussed:

- 'loafing around' and looking;
- finding newness while 'competing' with other writers;
- applying ideas from other arts, such as painting or music.

Think also about 'compressing' language and consider what T S Eliot said about the language of poetry – that if language in its usual forms cannot express the exact meanings that we want it must be *dislocated* into meaning.

Now select something common and everyday (after all, there are few things more common and everyday than butchers' and grocers' shops and dogs) and try to look at them in *a new* way. *It doesn't matter how outlandish or initially daft what you start writing is*.

Don't bother about form as you write EXCEPT that you may find the unrhymed couplet Craig Raine uses peculiarly apt for this sort of observation.

Like all the work produced in these assignments, what you do is meant for sharing with both group and class.

First Stage

When talking about how *In the Kalahari Desert* was written, Craig Raine once more said the poet is a focus for 'disparate experience'. To see a connection between the missionary story and the man saying 'Manchester' for any word he could not read seems logically absurd but, in the context, exactly right for the narrative.

Here is an extract from the original story of the missionaries:

TRIBULATION

Saturday, March 3rd, 1860. All are now down with this nasty, slow fever, with the exception of Roger and myself and Conate. Every one of the Helmores, poor things, so that one cannot help the other.

Malatsi and Monaisi we found when we arrived here quite safe, which much rejoiced our hearts. They have both, however, been ill all the time they have been here, and last evening after severe struggling, Malatsi breathed his last. Oh, we are very grieved! When the other men return home and carry to his friends the sad tidings of his death, alas, how will their hearts bleed! He has been so faithful to us of late, and of dear Baby he was so fond, which made me like him none the less. Roger and Conate attended his funeral, which took place a few hours after his death.

'No useless coffin enclosed his breast,
Nor in sheet, nor in shroud, they laid him,
But he lay, like a Becuan taking his rest, With just his kaross around him.'

Sekeletu has sent me a girl for a nursemaid and a comfort it is indeed to me, as my hands are not so tied. Baby seems very fond of her and now I can devote my time to the poor invalids.

Wednesday, March 7th. As Roger went to look round at the invalids this evening, he found dear little Henry cold in death.He communicated the sad information to his father, who bore the trial with marked calmness; his mother has not been told. Oh, how fond she was of him! And a sweeter child there certainly could not be. Roger had the dear little fellow removed at once and sewn up in a piece of carpeting. He was hastily buried by the side of Malatsi.

Oh, how I do wish we could get away from here, especially for dear Baby's sake. She looks pale and does not seem so well as she did. Roger too is failing now.

Thursday, March 8th. To-day have been ill myself and dear Baby too, and have not been able to help the others at all.

Friday, March 9th. Ah, Providence, how mysteriously art Thou dealing with us! My own sweet little one has to-day taken her flight from us. I saw a change in her countenance this morning and determined to keep her in my arms altogether. She took no food yesterday. Roger suffered much this morning from oppression of the chest, and just before midday wished for a cold sheet. I refused help at first, as I saw my precious one was dying, but on finding it really needed, I laid her on the mattress for a few minutes, while I served Roger.

Here is the poem itself.

In the Kalahari Desert

The sun rose like a tarnished
looking-glass to catch the sun

and flash His hot message
at the missionaries below –

Isabella and the Rev. Roger Price,
and the Helmores with a broken axle

left, two days behind, at Fever Ponds.
The wilderness was full of home:

a glinting beetle on its back
struggled like an orchestra

with Beethoven. The Hallé,
Isabella thought and hummed.

Makololo, their Zulu guide,
puzzled out the Bible, replacing

words he didn't know with Manchester.
Spikenard, alabaster, Leviticus,

were Manchester and Manchester.
His head reminded Mrs Price

of her old pomander tuck with cloves,
forgotten in some pungent tallboy.

The dogs drank under the wagon
with a far away clip-clopping sound,

and Roger spat into the fire,
leaned back and watched his phlegm

like a Welsh rarebit
bubbling on the brands …

When Baby died, they sewed her
in a scrap of carpet and prayed,

with milk still darkening
Isabella's grubby button-through.

Makololo was sick next day
and still the Helmores didn't come.

the outspanned oxen moved away
at night in search of water,

were caught and goaded on
to Matabele water-hole –

nothing but a dark stain on the sand.
Makololo drank vinegar and died.

Back they turned for Fever Ponds
and found the Helmores on the way …

Until they got within a hundred yards,
the vultures bobbed and trampolined

around the bodies, then swirled
a mile above their heads

like scalded tea leaves.
The Prices buried everything –

all the tattered clothes and flesh,
Mrs Helmore's bright chains of hair,

were wrapped in bits of calico
then given to the sliding sand.

'In the beginning was the Word' –
Roger read from Helmore's Bible

found open at St John.
Isabella moved her lips,

'The Word was Manchester'.
Shhh, shhh, the shovel said, Shhh …

In your groups, discuss and then list similarities and then differences between the two. Stop when you have reached three of each.

I don't know what you would have put. You might have thought it too obvious to put 'One's in prose and one's in verse' but I would think that's a very important point to put down straight away because everything else springs from it.

Among the similarities I would have put:

- the events in the story;
- the overpowering feeling of sadness.

However, I would have felt very doubtful about the second because though both transmit sadness, the sadness of the poem is of a very different nature.

- Where does the difference lie?

I think the clue lies in Craig Raine's interview, where he says: 'What gives the poem feeling is the notion of 'Manchester', the notion of where you should be.'

The wilderness is full of home.

So Isabella Price's sadness springs from losing those nearest to her while they were doing what she was convinced was right.

Craig Raine's sadness comes from seeing her endeavour as futile because she was in the wrong place. What they were doing was alien to where they were. Makalolo's reading 'Manchester' for hard words becomes a central image for this futility.

All the differences spring from this.

First Stage

What Craig Raine says about borrowing from different art forms and about cubist painting when he discusses *The Butcher* is also true about *A Martian Sends a Postcard Home*.

He also says of this poem, 'The reader has to decode what is going on from the clues given … but there are rules and there are solutions …'

Craig Raine

A Martian Sends a Postcard Home

Caxtons are mechanical birds with many
wings
and some are treasured for their markings –

they cause the eyes to melt
or the body to shriek without pain.

I have never seen one fly, but
sometimes they peck on the hand.

Mist is when the sky is tired of flight
and rests its soft machine on ground:

then the world is dim and bookish
like engravings under tissue paper.

Rain is when the earth is television.
It has the property of making colours
darker.

Model T is a room with the lock inside –
a key is turned to free the world.

for movement, so quick there is a film
to watch for anything missed.

But time is tied to the wrist
or kept in a box, ticking with impatience.

In homes, a haunted apparatus sleeps,
that snores when you pick it up.

If the ghost cries, they carry it
to their lips and soothe it to sleep

with sounds. And yet, they wake it up
deliberately, by tickling with a finger.

Only the young are allowed to suffer
openly. Adults go to a punishment room

with water but nothing to eat.
they lock the door and suffer the noises

alone. No one is exempt
and everyone's pain has a different
smell.

At night, when all the colours die,
they hide in pairs

and read about themselves –
in colour, with their eyelids shut.

In your groups, read silently and to each other the poem so that you know them well.

Craig Raine talks about one of the images he uses – the lavatory as a 'punishment room'. He says that even when you've worked out what it is, you won't forget the 'punishment room' association – there will always be an 'eerie' feeling about a lavatory.

This comes close to a basic and essential point about all images and metaphors. They should be 'reversible'; the thing the metaphor is describing should be clear – but so should the thing used to describe it. Each should illuminate the other.

In his poem *The Express* Stephen Spender describes a train leaving a station, running through suburbs until, before reaching open country, it passes a cemetery:

The heavy page of death.

This is a wonderful image for the whole panorama of the gravestones in a cemetery seen from above out of a carriage window. It's difficult not to recall this line, once you have read it in its context, whenever you see a graveyard. It has said something important about a way of looking at such a thing. But the word 'page' has worked in a different way: it is difficult now, at some level or other, not to associate the page of a book with a gravestone.

- In your groups, discuss the following points:

In both the poems printed above, how far are the central ideas reversible? – that is, how far do the perceptions of the Martians about us alter or modify our views about ourselves and our cars?

Second Stage

This activity brings work on all these poems together and provides a format for your own writing.

In the Kalahari Desert is a poem composed from an original piece of prose. So is *The Butcher*. *A Martian Sends a Postcard Home* is a succession of skewed images.

Here is a joke.

A man visiting a farm saw in the pig-sty a pig with a wooden leg.

'Why has that pig got a wooden leg' he asked the farmer.

'That is a wonderful pig,' said the farmer. 'One night the farm caught fire. That pig woke up, called the fire brigade and rescued us all from a blazing house.'

'Wonderful,' said the man. 'But why has he got a wooden leg?'

'That pig, said the farmer, 'learned to read. He taught all the piglets and then he taught my own children.'

'Fantastic' said the man. 'But why has he got a wooden leg?'

'That pig,' said the farmer, 'rescued my wife and mother-in-law when they fell in the pond. He jumped in, and brought them out single-handed, then gave them both the kiss of life.'

'Brilliant,' said the man. 'But why has he got a wooden leg?'

'Well, when you've got a pig like that,' said the farmer 'you don't want to eat him all at once.'

Here are two poems based on that old joke. The first is by John Mole.

The Three-Legged Pig

A pair of statesmen walking in the world
Saw only what they wanted to until
Their path was crossed by a three-legged
pig
wobbling a little but still coping well.

Good sir they said, hailing the peasant
Who, proprietorially, followed after,
What a splendid pig you have, but why
...?
He interrupted them with splendid
peasant laughter.

Sires, indeed you speak the truth. This
pig
Has, in its time, from fire and flood
And other accidents delivered me
In sundry ways. This pig is great and
good.

The statesmen, knowing they beheld a
wonder,
Wondered, while the peasant, like a
peasant, needed to get on.

Craig Raine

But why three legs? they asked him. Why
So maimed or incompletely formed, your
paragon?

He looked at them, in turn, amazed, as if
to ask
Which of such wise men was the greater
dunce
then answered When you find a pig as
marvellous as this
You don't eat it all at once.

The second is by John Cotton.

The leg of a pig

They gave it to Dolly
Because she was jolly –

The leg of a pig
The leg of a pig.

They gave it to Louisa
Because it would please her -

The leg of a pig
The leg of a pig.

They gave it to Berty
Because he was flirty –

The leg of a pig
The leg of a pig.

They gave it to Peggy
Because she was leggy –

The leg of a pig
The leg of a pig.

They gave it to Alice
to take to the Palace –

The leg of a pig
The leg of a pig.

They gave it to Prunella
To give to a fella –

The leg of a pig
The leg of a pig.

They gave it to Mary
Although she was wary –

The leg of a pig
The leg of a pig.

They gave it to Clare
Because she would share –

The leg of a pig
The leg of a pig.

They gave to to Jerry
Because he was merry –

The leg of a pig
The leg of a pig.

They gave it to Oscar
For his singing of Tosca –

The leg of a pig
The leg of a pig.

They gave it to Dawn
Whose knickers were torn –

The leg of a pig
The leg of a pig.

They gave it to Faye
Who gave it away –

The leg of a pig
The leg of a pig.

Both respond to the original joke in different ways and produce completely different poems.

John Cotton is interested in the idea of the leg of pork, which we only know about at the end of the pig joke because it is clear by then that it has been replaced on the pig by the wooden leg. What happened to it? Who was it passed on to?

John Mole is interested in the owner; the sagacious peasant with his country common sense too much for the sophisticated philosophers of high civilisation – he turns the joke into a sort of fable.

Both poets are doing on a small scale what Craig Raine is doing in *The Butcher* and – on a larger scale – in *In the Kalahari Desert*.

There was another, rather feeble, joke current a few years ago. Here it is. A flying saucer landed on earth right next to a garage and filling station. Fifty Martians disembarked and set out to meet the natives.

It was the dead of night and the place was deserted. But when the Martians reached the forecourt of the garage, at last they saw them. The Chief Martian went up to a pump selling unleaded petrol and said, 'Take me to your leader'.

In this bald narrative is a hint of Craig Raine's 'skewing' of view; there are possibilities of treatment which can be humorous, can be menacing (the alien invader), can be frightening (what scary, advanced creatures are these? – this could be thought by the Martians as well as by earthlings), can be rather pathetic (the poor deluded Martians). However, there is also a hint of the central idea of *In The Kalahari Desert* – being in the wrong place. Perhaps the Martians are in as much danger as Isabella Price.

You might look again at the end of the joke and ask; 'what happens next?'

- What do the Martians do when they don't get a reply?
- What if they do get a reply? What if there is some deep understanding between Martians and petrol pumps we mere humans know nothing of?
- Can the joke be continued beyond its punchline in a way the pig joke probably can't?

Ask these questions – and others – of the prose text to draw extra significance out of it so that you start thinking of the same sort of statement in verse that Craig Raine made in *The Martian sends a Postcard Home*.

Third Stage

In your groups or individually, attempt a poem, using whatever form you like, with the 'Take me to your leader' joke above as the subject. You can interpret the task as you wish; in this assignment are printed several sorts of possible responses to prose passages and you can follow whatever line you wish.

- When you are reasonably sure the time has come to abandon your work, then, as always, there should be a sharing and celebration of what has been done.

Vernon Scannell is a poet who challenges the all-too-common stereotypes of 'The Poet' as a bespectacled wimp who finds consolation in books for his lack of physical strength and prowess at games, and 'The Sportsman' (particularly if he is a boxer) as a semi-literate Neanderthal with an IQ in single figures.
Born in 1922, Vernon was a soldier in the Gordon Highlanders during the Second World War, and was wounded in Normandy. After the war he attended Leeds University where he as Captain of Boxing and Northern Universities Champion at welterweight, middleweight and cruiserweight. He also boxed professionally and travelled with a fairground boxing booth for a time.
He has written poetry, criticism, children's books, two volumes of autobiography and an account of his experiences as a 'Poet-in-residence', *A Proper Gentleman.*
Vernon is a member of the Royal Society of Literature, and was awarded a Civil List Pension in 1980 for his services to Literature.

Interview with
VERNON SCANNELL
by Mick Gowar

From a very early age – and by early I mean eight or nine – the only thing I was determined to do was write. Writing was what I liked to do, and although I had all sorts of other interests as a boy, reading and writing were my first and main interests. So while all the other boys of my age were doing healthy, sensible things like climbing trees, I was writing stories in Woolworths exercise books about pirates and outlaws – obviously based on the kind of thing I was reading.

I went to an elementary school in the thirties, and poetry was used – I wouldn't say taught – either punitively or as a kind of memory trainer. You had to learn certain poems off by heart, or if you did something fairly heinous the teacher might make you write out *Daffodils* ten times as a punishment.

I didn't take to poetry until I'd left school, when I was about fifteen or sixteen. I remember being in a second-hand bookshop in Aylesbury, and looking for something to read. I was browsing along the 'very cheap' shelf – everything threepence – and I picked up *The Methuen Book of Modern Verse* and found myself reading it with enjoyment. So I bought it, and I kept that copy for years. It contained a lot of mediocre Georgian verse, but there was also some Thomas Hardy, some W B Yeats, and some Siegfried Sassoon. It was Sassoon's poems which grabbed me at first – poems like *Counter Attack* and the poem about the soldier dying in a military hospital. They amazed me; I hadn't realised that you could write poems about such things as going over the top in war.

Once I started reading poetry, I became almost obsessed with finding out more about it. I didn't have anyone who could guide me, so I went to the library and got out all those chatty, Georgian books about books. But I enjoyed them, and they did point me in the way of some good poets: I read Eliot, for example, when I was fifteen or sixteen. I couldn't make much of his poems, but I enjoyed them all the same. And this is a fascinating aspect of poetry, as Eliot himself says in one of his essays: 'poetry can communicate before it is understood.' I'm sure that ninety per cent of what I read I didn't understand, in the sense of being able to paraphrase it. If somebody had asked me then what many of the poems I was reading were about, I would have said: 'I don't really know. I just like the feel , and the noise it makes.'

I joined the army when I was eighteen, and finally came out in 1945 by demobolising myself – in other words, I was a deserter. I hated the army. I'd been wounded in Normandy, and when the war in Europe ended – VE day – I was convalescent. I couldn't wait to hang around for de-mob, so I just cleared off – I'd had enough.

I came to live in Leeds; and it was while I was on the run that I really started to find out about reading and writing, and I also began to publish my poems in magazines. A lot of the stuff I was writing at the time was fairly trivial, but I was learning all the time. My main guide at the time was another anthology, *The Albatross Book of English Verse*.

It had a little appendix about poetic forms. It was very elementary, but it covered the main prescribed literary forms like the rondeau, the rondel, the ballade, the villanelle, the sonnet and so on. And this was a revelation to me; I didn't know anything about such things.

At this time also I was introduced to the Professor of English at Leeds University who gave me a place to read English. But I only did a year. Somebody must have given me away, because the police suddenly descended on me and I was taken back to my regimental depot in Aberdeen and court martialled.

At the court martial, I decided to defend myself. I explained to the Board that I hated the army, and the one thing I wanted to be was a writer. I said that I knew that if I stayed in the army I'd be finished. The court martial president, a colonel, said: 'What sort of writer?' And I said: 'A poet.' Their response was: 'Send him to a psychiatrist.' They'd decided I must be mad!

Looking back, I realise it was the cleverest thing I could have said because I was sent to an army psychiatrist, then to a mental hospital in Birmingham, and then given a medical discharge. The official diagnosis was 'anxiety neurosis' – i.e. incurably insane. So I came out and carried on writing.

I think I knew, even at the time, that my early poems really weren't very good. They were pastiches of poems I liked and admired – not even that sometimes. There was a struggle in some of them to really say something, but that was all. I hadn't found a voice of my own.

I think it's what happens to most, if not all young poets unless they're very exceptional. I think most young people begin by writing the kind of poems they admire. They read a poet, or poets, and say: 'By God! That's marvellous – I want to write like that!' After a couple of years of struggling, I realised that's not the way to do it: you don't sit down to write a poem like a poem by Eliot or Auden; you sit down and try to tell the truth.

I don't mean by truth just historical fact, I mean the truth about your response to the experience you're writing about. In other words, you mustn't inflate or distort your response; you mustn't squeeze more emotional juice out of the situation than naturally resides in it. A lot of poets succumb to that; they over-do it, they play to the gallery. In fact, they tell lies about their feelings.

I'm very suspicious about the free forms, about free verse. I'm not naive enough to think that free verse doesn't exist, but I sympathise with Eliot when he says in his essay on free verse: 'No verse is free for the man who wants to do a good job.' He's acknowledging that there is such a thing as free verse, but pointing out that it's a great deal less free than most people seem to think. A great deal of it, I think, isn't verse at all. I know Auden felt that too. He said, quoting Claudel I think: 'Anybody who finds that the demands of poetic form are restricting and inhibiting will never make a poet.' Too many young poets say: 'I can't do that. I can't write in metre, I can't write in stanzas – I must let it flow out.' But of course poetry doesn't just flow out.

But metre and rhyme are not what makes poetry what it is. These are devices which are available to the poet, and I think he would be a fool to ignore them. Of course young children think that anything that rhymes and has a sort of jog-trot, de-da-de-da metre is a poem. Not only children. I heard a disc jockey the other day saying: 'I'm going to read a poem from a listener ...' and then reciting it. Of course, it wasn't a poem, it was some terrible piece of doggerel: 'I've always loved you dearest Pete/ I'd even kiss your smelly feet.'

You see, the big mistake people make is in thinking that doggerel is an inferior form of poetry. It isn't.

Doggerel is the very opposite of poetry. When a poet uses language, he uses language with no clear idea of where it's going to lead him. Not with prose. The prose writer normally has some idea of what he wants to say; he's articulating preconceived ideas. But when I sit down to write a poem, the poem isn't already clear in my mind. I start with some kind of experience – either personal, or something I've read or heard – and I will have to explore the experience using language and poetic techniques. And ideally the poem will lead me into areas which will surprise me.

A good example of that is *A Case Of Murder*. At the time I wrote that poem I was living in a village in Dorset. I used to go into the local pub, and one of the regulars was a noisy, jovial extrovert sort of chap – always making bad jokes and guffawing. But one evening when I went into the pub he was very quiet, so much so that I walked over to where he was sitting and said to him, 'Do you feel alright? – You're so quiet this evening.' And eventually he told me what was the matter.

That afternoon, he and his wife had gone into the nearest town to do the week's shopping, and they'd left their son, Alan, at home playing. When they got back, they called Alan down from his room to have tea but he wouldn't come. They called again; he still wouldn't come down. When they went upstairs the found he'd locked himself in his room.

When they finally coaxed him out, he was clearly very upset. Finally, he admitted to his mother that while they'd been out he'd accidentally killed the cat. Those were the very words he used: 'accidentally killed the cat.'

And the man in the pub was saying to me: 'My boy's a monster! ... who's he going to kill next?

And I said: 'I shouldn't worry too much about it. It could have been some kind of accident ...' But yet, all the time I was thinking: Yes, I'd be a bit worried if one of my kids had accidentally killed the cat. How on earth do you kill a cat accidentally?

He never mentioned it again, but I kept thinking about this boy killing the cat: How the hell did he do it? Why did he do it? And at the same time I was reading *The Informed Heart*, which is a book by Bruno Bettelheim, a psychologist who actually survived one of the Nazi death camps. He kept himself sane by using his professional skills to observe the SS methods: the systematic humiliations; how they depersonalised the prisoners and robbed them of their identities until they could be lead, literally, like lambs to the slaughter. It's a fascinating and horrible book.

So I was thinking a lot about sadism, and a lot about guilt – the guilt of the German people. And that came into the poem, too. It's very much a poem about guilt and sadism: how the cat stirs sadistic feelings in the boy which he surrenders to; the boy's guilt and remorse when he kills the cat – maybe half-accidentally.

But what the end means is up to the

reader to decide, because I had no idea the poem would end like that when I started writing it. When the cat got into the cupboard, and you could hear it purring for years and years; when the giant monster came out of the cupboard to get him – I was surprised by what I'd written. I thought I could see what it meant: putting the cat in the cupboard was repressing guilt, but sooner or later it comes out to get him; the cupboard being a symbol for his consciousness. But I was actually reading it as if somebody else had written it. I was saying to myself: 'What does that mean?' And that's what I meant by the exploratory nature of poetry.

Nettles is a poem about parents' impotence in the face of the fact of pain; the continuity of pain as part of the process of children growing up.

We were living in Surrey at the time, and at the bottom of our garden was a shed which had nettles behind it and John, my middle son, was playing in the garden one hot, summer afternoon. He was either naked, or he had on a pair of little swimming trunks, and he fell into the nettles. And I can remember him running up the garden, yelling like mad, covered in white blisters. And as it says in the poem, we calmed him down and then I went out with my hook and 'slashed in fury' at the nettles.

But one thing I notice now about the poem – that I was probably unconscious of when I first started to write it – is the amount of military imagery: 'Green spears ... regiment of spite ... fierce parade ... called up tall recruits ... pyre to burn the fallen ... my son would often feel sharp wounds.'

The poem was written in the early sixties, at the time of the Cuban missile crisis when a third world war looked well on the cards. I'm sure that when I wrote that poem I was worried about my children and what would happen to them if there was another war, and that crept into the poem through that choice of imagery.

Although I put a lot of emphasis on form, metre and traditional forms are things that can be learnt. But what is much more difficult and certainly more important than mastering techniques is to realise that when you are using language poetically you aren't writing about something, you're actually presenting the situation itself. Poets create events in language.

As I was saying earlier, prose talks about a subject and therefore the language of prose tends always to move towards the abstract. But in the finest poetry – at least from the Romantics on – very rarely are abstract words used. A perfect example of this is Thomas Hardy's poem *During Wind And Rain*. The poem is about the past; about how even the distant past can be more urgently present than the actual chronological present. It's about death, mortality, the process of ageing, time, and eternity. But there is not one abstract word in the whole poem. I've used a whole string of abstracts because I'm talking about it. All the people Hardy mentions in the poem are dead, but he never uses the word 'death'. He says: 'Down their carved names the raindrop ploughs.' And that's what I mean about creating an event and not just writing about it.

I would encourage any young writer to use imagery; to use their eyes, and to use their other senses too. Also, to be aware of words being exciting things. If you think of words as nothing more than ciphers to express our needs or to impart information then you will never write poetry.

Language is much more than that; words have magic power. I use that term hesitatingly because it sounds whimsical, but it's no accident that you never get a magic spell without it employing the techniques of poetry. Words also have their own special texture and density, taste and colour. And if you think of language as something exciting, then you're on your way to becoming a poet.

Publications

Poetry:

The Loving Game, Robson, 1975.
New and Collected Poems 1950-1980, Robson, 1980.
Winterlude, Robs, 1982.
Funeral Games, Robson, 1987.

Autobiography:

The Tiger And The Rose, Hamis Hamilton, 1971.
A Proper Gentleman, Robson, 1977.
An Argument of Kings, Robson, 1987.

Educational:

How To Enjoy Novels, Piatkus, 1984.
How To Enjoy Poetry, Piatkus, 1987.

Literary terms

Stanzas When describing the shape and pattern of a poem people often say verse when they mean stanza. A poet will often divide a poem into small regular groups of lines, and the correct name for these groups are stanzas. In formal rhymed poetry the stanza will also govern the metre and the pattern of rhymes. A stanza which almost everyone is familiar with is the limerick (see page 27), which is a one-stanza poem. Indeed, the conventions of the limerick not only given the metre and rhyme scheme, but also the sort of subject matter (it's hard to imagine anyone choosing to write about grief or love in a serious way in a limerick) and the way the plot or story is developed with a punch-line at the end. Edward Lear's limericks, for example, often seem disappointing to a modern reader because Lear normally doesn't provide a gag at the end but instead repeats the first line.

Many of the poetic forms talked about in the interview are formal stanzaic poems. Examples include villanelle (see p 45), triolet, (see p 45) and sonnet (see p 45).

Notes on the other forms Vernon Scannell uses can be found as follows:

ballade page 27, villanelle page 102, sonnet page 104.

Assignment 1

All the poets interviewed make the point very strongly that there was a stage in their becoming poets when they wrote like other poets; that, as Vernon Scannell says, they said, 'By God! That's marvellous – I want to write like that.'

However, though Vernon Scannell acknowledges that this was part of his development, he insists that – as an aim – it was wrong; that his wish to write a poem like someone else's didn't lead to writing a poem, but sitting down to write the truth did.

DISCUSSION

In your groups, consider the following matters:

- Is Vernon Scannell's attitude to previous poets different from those of the other poets interviewed?
- If it is, then in what way?

I don't know what you would have said but I would have to come up with the irritating answer,, 'It is and it isn't.' All the poets owe a debt to previous poets; all of them say how they tried to write like other poets before they found their own voice. I find it interesting that Vernon Scannell says he only wrote poetry when he tried to write the truth, as if he is rejecting all that went before. Craig Raine is quite close to this view, but Wendy Cope's attitude is different; she seems much more consciously connected to other poets and indeed gets most of her distinctiveness from it.

Here are two poems that Vernon Scannell mentions in his interview as examples of his craft – *A Case of Murder* and *Nettles*.

A Case of Murder

They should not have left him there alone,
Alone that is except for the cat.
He was only nine, not old enough
To be left alone in a basement flat,
Alone, that is, except for the cat.
A dog would have been a different thing,
A big gruff dog with slashing jaws,
But a cat with round eyes mad as gold,
Plump as a cushion with tucked-in paws –
Better have left him with a fair-sized rat!
But what they did was leave him with a cat.
He hated that cat; he watched it sit,
A buzzing machine of soft black stuff,
He sat and watched and he hated it,
Snug in its fur, hot blood in a muff,
And its mad gold stare and they way it sat
Crooning dark warmth: he loathed all that.
So he took Daddy's stick and he hit the cat.

Then quick as a sudden crack in glass
It hissed, black flash, to a hiding place
In the dust and dark beneath the couch,
And he followed the grin on his new-made face,
A wide-eyed, frightened snarl of a grin,
And he took the stick and he thrust it in,
Hard and quick in the furry dark.
the black fur squealed and he felt his skin
Prickle with sparks of dry delight.
Then the cat again came into sight,
Shot for the door that wasn't quite shut,

But the boy, quick too, slammed fast the door:
The cat, half-through, was cracked like a nut
And the soft black thud was dumped on the floor.
Then the boy was suddenly terrified
And he bit his knuckles and cried and cried;
But he had to do something with the dead thing there.
His eyes squeezed beads of salty prayer
But the wound of fear gaped wide and raw;
He dared not touch the thing with his hands
So he fetched a spade and shovelled it
And dumped the load of heavy fur
In the spidery cupboard under the stair
Where it's been for years, and though it died
Its grown in that cupboard and its hot low purr
Grows slowly louder year by year:
There'll not be a corner for the boy to hide
When the cupboard swells and all sides split
And the huge black cat pads out of it.

Nettles

My son aged three fell in the nettle bed.
'Bed' seemed a curious name for those green spears.
That regiment of spite behind the shed:
It was no place for rest. With sobs and tears
The boy came seeking comfort and I saw
White blisters beaded on his tender skin.
We soothed him till his pain was not so raw.
At last he offered us a watery grin.
And then I took my hook and honed the blade
And went outside and slashed in fury with it
Till not a nettle in that fierce parade
Stood upright any more. Next task: I lit
A funeral pyre to burn the fallen dead.
But in two weeks the busy sun and rain
Had called up tall recruits behind the shed:
My son would often feel sharp wounds again.

2

First Stage

In your groups, look carefully at these poems. Read them silently, read them aloud to each other several times until you feel you really know them. Don't worry about repetition becoming boring: these poems can well stand it.

When you feel you can, for the moment, gain no more from them, look back on your reading. What did you think?

I don't know what you would have said but I think I would have found *A Case of Murder* such a disturbing and powerful poem that I might have found difficulty in finishing a reading aloud of it.

Nettles I would have found great delight in – not at all because it is funny because it certainly isn't, but because of how Vernon Scannell makes the simple, honest and familiar emotion so clear and vivid that we share it at once. It is a very basic human feeling – that of wanting to lash out at something handy to blame (after all, the nettles are only being nettles).

Second Stage

Now look again at what Vernon Scannell says about how these poems are written. Here is Thomas Hardy's *During Wind and Rain* that he mentions.

During Wind and Rain

They sing their dearest songs –
He, she, all of them – yea,
Treble and tenor and bass,
And one to play;
With the candles mooning each face ....
Ah, no; the years O!
How the sick leaves reel down in throngs!
They clear the creeping moss –
Elders and juniors – aye,
Making the pathways neat
And the garden gay;
And they build a shady seat ....
Ah, no; the years, the years;
See, the white storm-birds wing across!

They are blithely breakfasting all –
Men and maidens – yea,
Under the summer tree,
With a glimpse of the bay,
While pet fowl come to the knee ....
Ah, no; the years O!
And the rotten rose is ripped from the wall.

They change to a high new house,
He, she, all of them – aye,
Clocks and carpets and chairs
On the lawn all day,
And brightest things that are theirs ....
Ah, no; the years, the years;
Down their carved names the rain-drop ploughs.

Vernon Scannell says of this poem: 'that's what I mean about creating an event, not writing about it.' About *A Case of Murder* he says, 'What the end means is up to the reader to decide because I had no idea the poem would end like that when I started writing it. About *Nettles* he says '… one thing I notice now about the poem – that I was probably unconscious of when I first started to write it – is the amount of military imagery …'

So Vernon Scannell seems to be saying that writing flows out in a way that he is unaware of and doesn't plan.

However, he also says he is suspicious of free verse and that 'too many young poets say …I must let it flow out. But of course poetry doesn't just flow out.'

DISCUSSION

In your groups, consider these points:

- Is Vernon Scannell contradicting himself?
- If you think he isn't, how can the two seemingly opposed ideas above be brought together?
- What does this have to do with what he says about Hardy's *During Wind and Rain*?

Well, it would be difficult to insist that Vernon Scannell is contradicting himself. There must be some other way in which not being aware of the implications or the outcomes of what you write as you write it is different from just 'letting it flow out.'

To find an answer we will look at his poem *Growing Pain* – not only the printed poem but also an earlier draft.

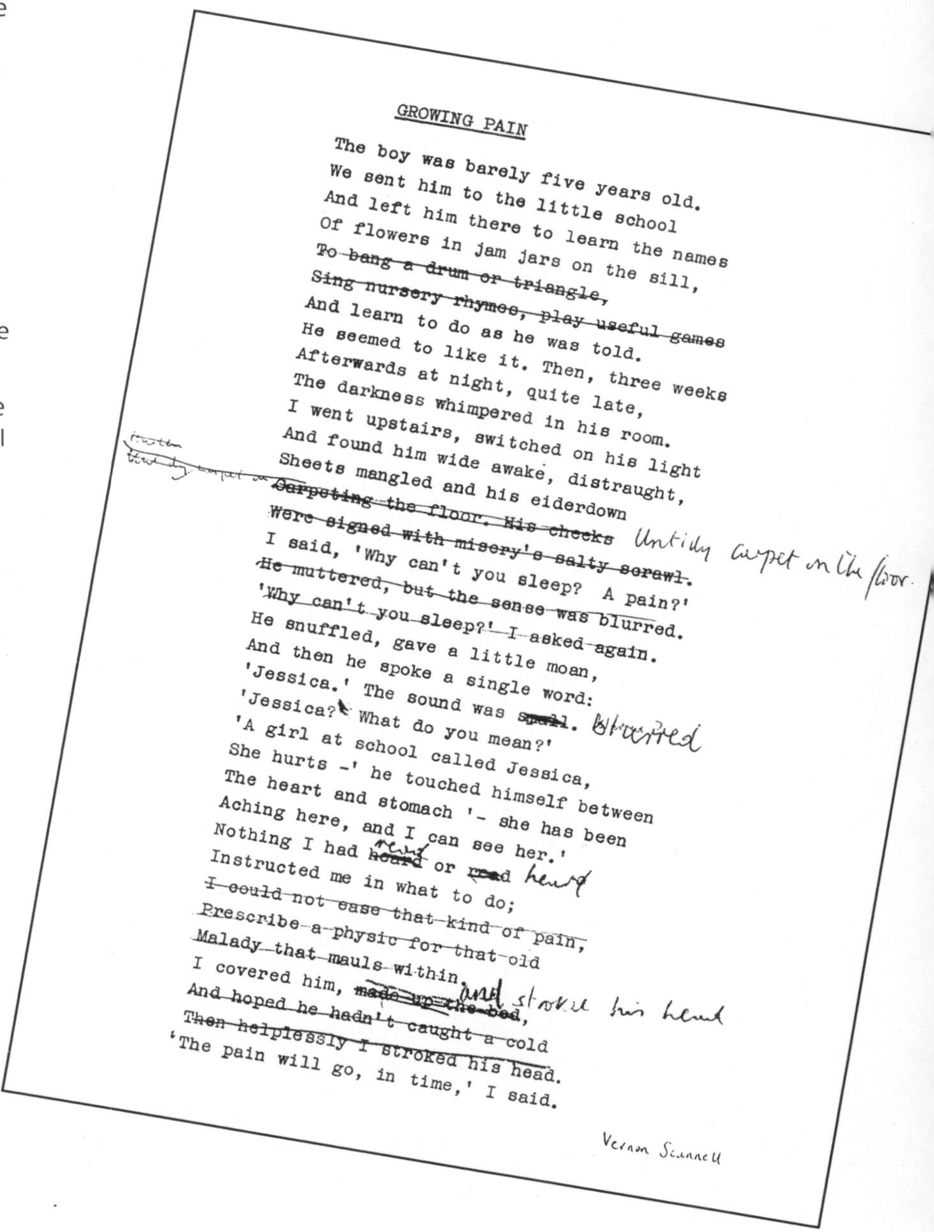
GROWING PAIN

The boy was barely five years old.
We sent him to the little school
And left him there to learn the names
Of flowers in jam jars on the sill,
~~To bang a drum or triangle,~~
~~Sing nursery rhymes, play useful games~~
And learn to do as he was told.
He seemed to like it. Then, three weeks
Afterwards at night, quite late,
The darkness whimpered in his room.
I went upstairs, switched on his light
And found him wide awake, distraught,
Sheets mangled and his eiderdown
~~Carpeting the floor. His cheeks~~
~~Were signed with misery's salty scrawl.~~ Untidy carpet on the floor.
I said, 'Why can't you sleep? A pain?'
~~He muttered, but the sense was blurred.~~
~~'Why can't you sleep?' I asked again.~~
He snuffled, gave a little moan,
And then he spoke a single word:
'Jessica.' The sound was ~~small~~. blurred
'Jessica? What do you mean?'
'A girl at school called Jessica,
She hurts –' he touched himself between
The heart and stomach '– she has been
Aching here, and I can see her.'
Nothing I had ~~heard~~ read or ~~read~~ heard
Instructed me in what to do;
~~I could not ease that kind of pain,~~
~~Prescribe a physic for that old~~
~~Malady that mauls within.~~
I covered him, ~~made up the bed,~~ and stroked his head
~~And hoped he hadn't caught a cold~~
~~Then helplessly I stroked his head.~~
'The pain will go, in time,' I said.

Vernon Scannell

Growing Pain

The boy was barely five years old.
We sent him to the little school
And left him there to learn the names
Of flowers in jam jars on the sill
And learn to do as he was told.
He seemed quite happy there until
Three weeks afterwards, at night,
The darkness whimpered in his room.
I went upstairs, switched on his light,
And found him wide awake, distraught,
Sheets mangled and his eiderdown
Untidy carpet on the floor.
I said, 'Why can't you sleep? A pain?'
He snuffled, gave a little moan,
And then he spoke a single word:
'Jessica.' The sound was blurred.
'Jessica? What do you mean?'
'A girl at school called Jessica,
She hurts –' he touched himself between
The heart and stomach '– she has been
Aching here and I can see her.'
Nothing I had read or heard
Instructed me in what to do.
I covered him and stroked his head.
'The pain will go, in time,' I said.

The first version is Vernon Scannell's own amended typescript. Already, before he makes the alterations by hand on this draft he has worked long and hard at the poem to reach what he probably thought was a finished draft. But now he works further on it and reduces it by eleven lines, from thirty-six to twenty-five. In other words, he axes nearly a third of the poem. Why?

In your groups, look carefully at the differences between the two texts. What do you find?

What I find is that he has compressed ideas and images. The poem was pretty compressed already. But he has excised two lines of things that happened at school, has left out the direct information that the boy was crying and got rid of a memorable term for love:

... *that old Malady that mauls within*.

The lines he has dumped are gone not because they are not good – 'misery's salty scrawl' is a marvellous description of crying – but because they don't directly help with the narrative.

So Vernon Scannell seems to be behaving more like a novelist. This redrafting is not quite the same as the redrafting done by Wendy Cope for *Rondeau Redouble,* which is devoted to getting the strict form right and the ideas in the most effective and sharpest-sounding order.

Third Stage

Look again in your groups at this first draft of *Growing Pain* and then at the final draft.

- As you do so, remember what all the poets have said about the importance of knowing about particular poetic forms
- Also remember what Vernon Scannell said of Hardy – that he is '... creating an event, not just writing about it.'
- And recall the question we started with; what is the difference between Vernon Scannell's unconscious mind expressing itself in ways he does not expect and '... letting it flow out'?

In your groups, read both drafts of the poem to each other. Let each group member perform it. Listen carefully to what you hear.

Then individually or as a group exercise, plot the rhyme-scheme in the faint draft – using the formula A-B-C etc. – thus: old/told A: school/B: names C (where has 'games' gone?). This may seem a puzzling exercise; there is a rhyming pattern because *old, sill, night*, etc. do have rhymes but lines two and three don't (though line three once did). Whatever pattern there is, is not at all regular except that the poem ends with a rhyming couplet.

Fourth Stage

- Listen to the poem as a whole again and see if you can detect other rhymes – words which echo within the lines.
- Look carefully at the first draft again. Note the alterations Vernon Scannell makes involving the particular words 'blurred', 'head' and 'heard'. Why does he make changes here? What effects does he get?
- Do you notice anything in particular about many of the rhyming words, both within and at the ends of lines?

There is a lot to be said in answer to all these questions and I am only going to venture a few observations. It seems to me that many of these words contain long soft vowel sounds and light consonants – 'blurred', 'heard', 'moan', 'hurts'. There are echoes of long vowel sounds throughout – 'I', 'sound', 'eiderdown', 'spoke', 'light', 'distraught' and many more, so many that they cannot be accidental.

Why?

There are many things which can be said about the connections between the sounds of words and feelings, in this poem and elsewhere. It is best to find out what they are by living through the poem – and remembering again what Vernon Scannell said about Hardy's *During Wind and Rain* – '… creating an event, not just writing about it.'

Here is what might be a clue to the process. Thomas Hardy's poem is about sadness at the inevitability of death at the end of life. Nowhere does he say, 'these are melancholy happenings and I am sad about them'. The sadness comes from the depiction of the scene and the effects of the words, the rhymes and the rhythms. Notice what words Vernon Scannell cuts out in his early draft – 'misery's salty scrawl' and 'the old/malady which mauls within'. These are the words which tell us what the emotion is. The words which are left enact the scene without telling us what to think. The poem speaks for itself and this is what Vernon Scannell means. His poem has spoken truer than he knew because it was written in a disciplined framework, not because he let it 'flow out'.

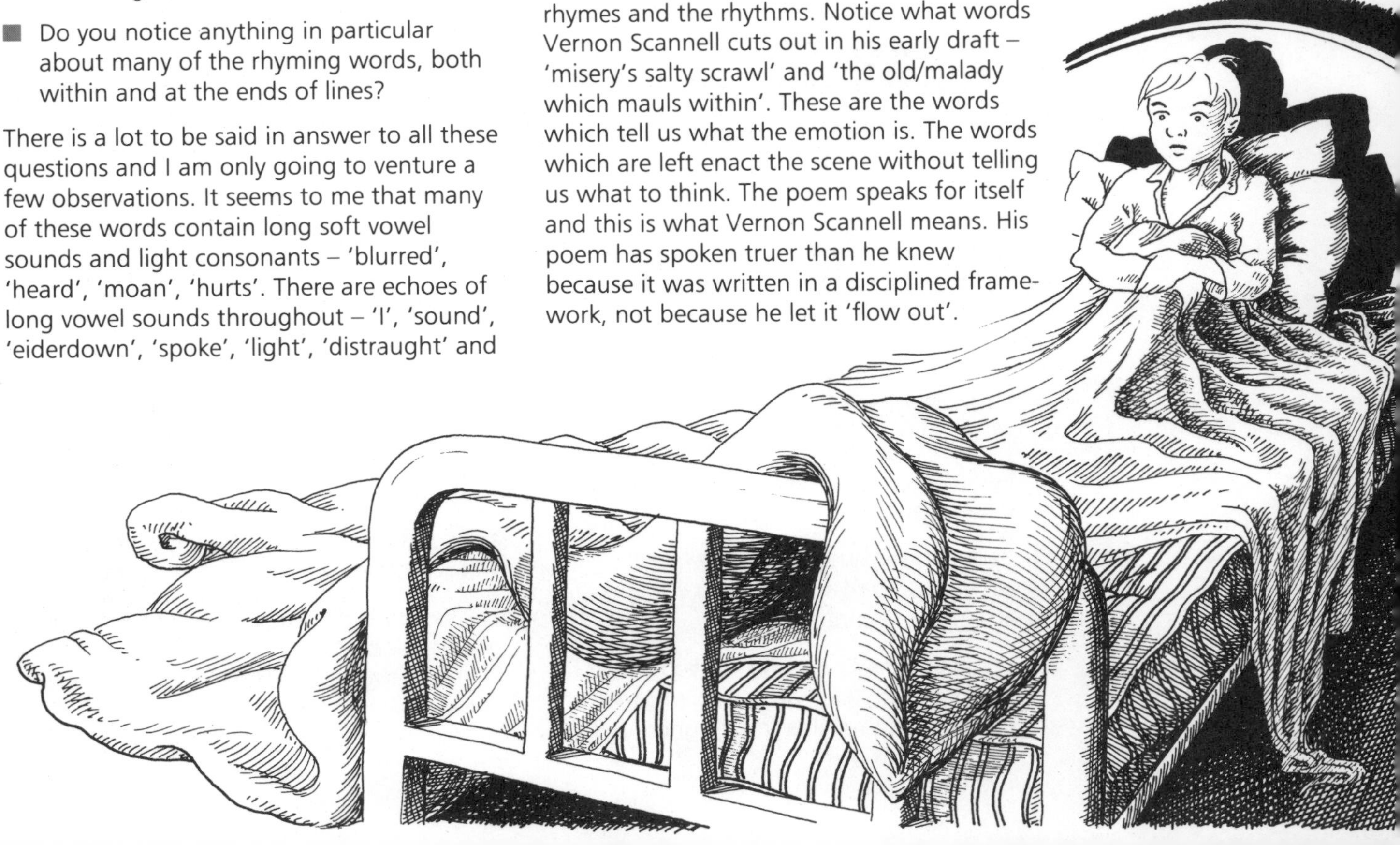

3

First Stage

All the poems by Vernon Scannell we have looked at have certain things in common.

- In your groups, name some.

I don't know what you would have said but one among several of the things that have occurred to me is that all three take little incidents – two directly experienced, one told – about children, recount them as narratives and then see general significance in them which is of importance to everybody.

It could be – and often has been – said that this is the whole business of the writer, in whatever genre: to see significance in ordinary things and express it. In the end, it is the significance which makes the writing worthwhile.

Second Stage

In your groups, look back to Assignment 4 based on Wendy Cope's interview. Here you were asked to reminisce so as to try and identify moments from the past which seemed to have within them some significance so they could be recaptured in verse. I said you might not ever finish that assignment. Events can't come crowding back to order and when they do they may seem to have no meaning whatever beyond themselves.

In the meantime, however, two things might have happened.

- Your memory worked in a 'delayed action' way and supplied you with events after the assignment
- Your subconscious mind worked away and has since told you the significance of things you remembered but ignored.

Something else might have happened as well.

- You thought of something but it was too painful to tell, let alone write about.

If you felt the third, remember these lines from a poem called *The Triple Fool* by the seventeenth-century poet John Donne:

Then as th'earth's inward narrow crooked lanes
Do purge sea water's fretfull salt away,
I thought, if I could draw my paines,
Through Rimes vexation, I should them allay.
Grief brought to numbers cannot be so fierce,
For he tames it that fetters it in verse.

Now, in your groups ask yourselves:

- Is this what Vernon Scannell did (and Wendy Cope in *Tich Miller*) – take 'pain' and 'tame' it by 'fettering it in verse'?
- Does this seem a good reason (among many others) to write?
- Could it be a reason for you to write?

Third Stage

John Donne's word 'fetter' is a good one to use to describe much of what Vernon Scannell says about the relationship of feeling with form.

In your groups:

- Look carefully at the account of forms in the POETRY NOTES.
- Either take the free verse poem you wrote for the *Tich Miller* assignment and attempt to turn it into a rhymed, regular form of your choice

Or look at the experience that has been boiling away unwritten since that assignment and attempt to turn it into a narrative verse, either free or regular.

Fourth Stage

In your groups and/or to the whole class, share your poems and be prepared to talk about them to each other.

This last assignment on an individual poet is a reading assignment. It unites a theme covered in the interviews and assignments with an important theme the poets have only touched upon by implication.

Theme 1 All the poets have talked about continuity, of looking at other poets, of their assumption and belief that they are members of a great company over the centuries.

These 2 Poetry can be funny, sad, private but also universal because poets speak for us all. There have been many different definitions of poetry: 'The expression of a society at its most sensitive point,' said F W Bateson. 'A criticism of life,' said Matthew Arnold. All the poets here would recognise the definitions. But see what the poet Shelley said in *A Defence of Poetry*:

'Poets are the unacknowledged legislators of the world'.

In other words, poets aren't private. They can see the truth before other people and they have the power to express the big issues. They don't have a hand in government, but they have a voice and should have an influence.

In Britain, we are different about this from some other countries. We tend to think of writers – novelists, dramatists, poets – as entertainers, while the people of power and action get on with the real work. Elsewhere it can be different – after all, in Czechoslovakia, a writer was let out of prison and became President.

But here, as Wilfred Owen said, 'All a poet can do today is warn'.

Here are two poems which bring these two themes together – continuity and membership of a great company and the right – and need – to warn about the big issues.

The first is by the nineteenth-century poet Matthew Arnold. *Dover Beach* was written at a time when Arnold felt pessimistic about the modern Victorian world.

Dover Beach

The sea is calm tonight,
The tide is full, the moon lies fair
Upon the straits; – on the French coast the light
Gleams, and is gone; the cliffs of England stand,
Glimmering and vast, out in the tranquil bay.
Come to the window, sweet is the night-air!
Only, from the long line of spray
Where the sea meets the moon-blanch'd land,
Listen! You hear the grating roar
Of pebbles which the waves draw back, and fling,
At their return, up the high strand,
Begin, and cease, and then again begin,
With tremulous cadence slow, and bring
The eternal note of sadness in.

Sophocles long ago
Heard it on the Aegaean, and it brought
Into his mind the turbid ebb and flow
Of human misery; we
Find also in the sound a thought,
Hearing it by this distant northern sea.

The Sea of Faith
Was once, too, at the full, and round earth's shore
Lay like the folds of a bright girdle furl'd.
But now I only hear
Its melancholy, long, withdrawing roar,
Retreating, to the breath
Of the night-wind down the vast edges drear
And naked shingles of the world.
Ah, love, let us be true
To one another! for the world, which seems
To lie before us like a land of dreams,
So various, so beautiful, so new,
Hath really neither joy, nor love, nor light,
Nor certitude, nor peace, nor help for pain;
And we are here as on a darkling plain
Swept with confused alarms of struggle and flight,
Where ignorant armies clash by night.

- Read this poem to each other in your groups.
- What did you make of it?

I don't know what you would have said; whole books have been written on this poem. But you might have found it depressing – even slightly frightening – in its view of what the world is becoming. Yet you might have found the line 'Ah, love, let us be true to one another' very cheering.

Here is another poem, written in 1980 by Vernon Scannell.

■ Read it to each other in your groups.

A Partial View

It floods the world, it surges like the sea,
Unnecessary suffering that men
Inflict on other men, and equally
Ubiquitous the pleasure felt by them,
Those specialists in pain who busily
Immerse themselves in grave research to
find
New strains and modes to benefit their
kind.
Steve Biko's agony was someone's joy
Who found delight in witnessing a mind
And body, both superior to his own,
Broken and wasted wantonly. Each slug
That smashes through the knee-cap of a
boy
In Ulster is a sweet addictive drug
To him who grasps the gun; the scream
or moan
Is transcendental music to the thug.
Neat bureaucrats of systematic death,
To outward view impassive and
stone-eyed,
Were tremulous and sticky underneath
Smart tunics when they practised
genocide.
When hanging by the neck was used to
cure
The anti-social habits of the poor
And solve the problems of the men who
fill
From passion, lunacy or greed, forever,
A mob of eager aspirants would fill
The market-place petitioning for the
prize,
The office of Chief Executioner.
We live in violent times and always did.
The history of the globe is soaked in
blood
And excrement,, and we do not improve.
My local paper recently described
An incident in a Wessex seaside town:
A little boy, five years of age, was found
Howling in a public lavatory.
His prick had been cut off, this surgery
Performed by one young man assisted by
Two comrades who held fast their
helpless patient.
The operation done, they speedily
Departed on the rasping motorbikes.
This scene poisons the sick imagination:
Their laughter darkening the afternoon
Like burning tyres. Black stench. Say
what you like,
There's not a day that breaks that is not
strewn
With pain and wreckage, smeared with
blood and pus,
Reeling with rage and blind brutality.
Of course I know this is a partial view
That fails to take account of those, like
us,
Who represent the great majority,
The decent who deplore such cruelty.
For every act of violence we could find
A score of altruistic deeds performed;
Most people fundamentally, are kind
And hate to see the humblest creature
harmed.
If true it is quite understandable,
This pit for the poor, solicitude
For those who are deprived and are
unable
To help themselves; in offering them aid
We re-affirm the human; our reponse
Is rational and we are sane, although
Precariously so. How can we know
That our apparently well-balanced stance
Is set upon foundations firmly laid?
Who knows what levelling stroke is, even
now,
Being planned by human evil or the
weather?

Vernon Scannell

Indignation may have steamed the glass,
Our vision lost the power of seeing how
Atrocities need not dress up on leather;
Not every yobbo mutters broken type
Nor swings a fist with knuckles made of brass.
The public outrage cannot be concealed;
There is a kind of candour, though not willed,
In blatant executions in broad daylight
That might deflect attention from the plight
Of tortured victims in quiet drawing-rooms,
From libraries where prisoners are grilled
By soft-voiced experts, ruthless and polite,
And from those murders in the afternoons
To chink of teacup and the chime of spoons.
It drowns the children's weeping in the night.
God help us, who are we to act the judge
When fantasies of vengeance warm the blood
And we are gripped by passions we condemn?
We live in violent times and always did.
Tenants of this universal slum
We clamour for a more salubrious home
Yet know that what we are is where we live
And vice-versa. Mankind has not become
Much wiser in its umpteenth million year,
Or gentler, or more generous or just;
More sly perhaps and hypocritical.
Napalm and laser-beam replace the spear,
The ignorant plague gives way to clever dust,
Our language laced by words like 'overkill'.
No nation yet has ever won a war
Yet wars are fought despite the monstrous cost;
Some murders it would seem are ethical.
What is there then to do or say about it?
We could of course anticipate the end
Which mocks all striving yet without which life
Would be unthinkable and all its treasures
Dross, the oldest enemy and friend,
Meet him by way of bullet, gas or knife
Or kinder overdose; but these are measures
Providing answers only to the blind,
Completing the mad circle of destruction.
The rich can build elaborate defences,
Surround themselves with various distractions,
Enlist a corps of connoisseurs and ponces
To cater for their still discerning senses
Or, less sophisticated, they can choose
The blurred and stumbling cul-de-sac of booze
To join at last the swelling exodus
Of immigrants who daily put to sea
Bound for the Happy Isles and lives of bliss,
Utopias of total lunacy.
Our graveyards and insane asylums bear
Plain witness to the popularity
Of stratagems like these. And as for prayer,
The chance of supernatural intercession
Must be at least unlikely, and indeed
Why should God – whose notions of compassion
Have often seemed ironic – intercede?
So what is left? The little consolations
Of human love? Take her to the seaside,
Stand by the window in the sweet night air
And promise to be true to one another.

Yes, why not? But there is something more.
While you stand there swapping vows and kisses,
Hearing the ocean's long withdrawing roar,
Remember that you could be listening to
More varied music than that salty cadence.
When sick and hot from too much of the world
Immerse yourself in pure consoling art,
Press forehead to the coolness of a fugue,
Invite the wordless message to unfold
Its insubstantial scrolls of filigree.
There's always music. But should you wish to hear
The less transcendent language of the tongue
Then choose the harmonies of poetry
Which builds small barricades against confusion;
Or better, be a dancer at their wedding,
Discover there a nostrum for despair,
And unexpected joy that drowns foreboding,
And find yourself, with almost no surprise,
Accepting everything, rejoicing even
That all is as it is, not otherwise;
Though when the music fades and meanings blur,
The hordes remass, you turn again to her
To whom you might conceivably be true
As she, against the odds, might be to you.

- What do you make of it?

I don't know what you would have said but I know that I find it profoundly disturbing, even revolting, in its detail. But he is saying things about our world which have to be said.

I also would have noticed, especially at the end, a lot of reference to *Dover Beach*.

- What else but a poem could say these things effectively?
- Why should Vernon Scannell refer so clearly to *Dover Beach*?

Perhaps you would feel as I do that Vernon Scannell is doing exactly what a poet should. He is an 'unacknowledged legislator of the world' in this poem because he is defining what ought to be the way of the world and at the same time showing how it actually works. This poem – like all literature – is reflective: it 'creates' events: the poet does not just 'write about them'.

I am sure also that here Vernon Scannell does regard himself, as do the other poets, as part of a great tradition. Because he shares a pessimistic view of the world with Matthew Arnold he has consciously written a 'updating' of *Dover Beach*.

In this way, poetry – and all other literature – constantly develops and renews itself.

Comparative Assignment

All the poets interviewed in this book are very sure that poetry is a disciplined craft with its own rules and you can only break them when you have mastered them.

Roger McGough tells how when he first started writing, he '... copied the forms I was reading, like the French ballade. But than as I read more, I became aware of other sorts of poems; other ways of setting a poem out. And that's a very exciting part of becoming a poet: experimenting ...'

Wendy Cope says '... one of the things I like about using traditional forms and metres is that there are rules to guide you, but you still need to have a feeling for it. I'm not an expert on scansion ... I think it's more important to read and to use your ears.'

Craig Raine says '... you need to know about rhyme and metre in order to appreciate what it is to – say – break metre.'

Vernon Scannell tells how his *Albatross Book of English Verse* told him '... about poetic forms ... (which) ... covered the main prescribed literary forms like the rondeau, the rondel, the ballade, the villanelle, the sonnet and so on. And this was a revelation to me.'

In the assignments on the four poets, you are only twice asked to write in a particular form – the limerick and the haiku. This assignment is aimed at giving you understanding of what some of the other forms are – and also why they exist as separate forms; what they are suitable for and what they are not. It would, after all be difficult to write a serious poem about death as a limerick. You could try, but no-one would take it very seriously.

First Stage

We are going to look at three poetic forms: the villanelle, the triolet and the two types of sonnet. We are going to take one example of each in scrambled form and reconstruct it. To do this, you must read carefully the description of the form which follows and also how to describe the rhyme scheme.

Rhyme scheme – give each line ending a letter of the alphabet and show repeated lines as capital letters: for example, this poem by Rudyard Kipling (1865-1936) can have its rhyme scheme displayed thus –

The Way through the Woods

They shut the road through the woods a
Seventy years ago. b
Weather and rain have undone it again (c) c
And now you would never know b
There was once a road through the woods a
Before they planted the trees. d
It is underneath the coppice and heath (e) e
And the thin anemones. d
Only the keeper sees d
That where the ring-dove broods, a
And the badgers roll at ease, d
There was once a road through the woods. a

Yet if you enter the woods a
Of a summer evening late, b
When the night air cools on the trout-ringed pools c
Where the otter whistles his mate b
(They fear not men in the woods, a
Because they see so few.) d
You will hear the beat of a horse's feet, (e) e
And the swish of a skirt in the dew, a
Steadily cantering through a
The misty solitudes, a
As though they perfectly knew d
The old lost road through the woods ... a
But there is no road through the woods. a

VILLANELLE

This is the definition given in the Literary Terms, page 45:

'It is thought to have originated in Italy in the late 1400's. The name means 'rural song' although modern villanelles deal with a wide variety of subjects. Only two end rhymes are allowed and the first and third lines must be repeated according to a strict pattern throughout the poem. There are six stanzas in all: five stanzas of three lines each and a final stanza of four lines.'

Look at the setting out of the rhyme scheme for *The Way through the Woods.* Note that when there are two letters on the same line there is an internal rhyme ('rain/again', 'cools/pools'). Look also at the last line. Did you notice that it is an extra line, making a thirteen-line verse after one of twelve lines? What effect does this give? The rhyme at the end is repeated: the line is nearly (but significantly not quite) repeated and though I have marked the rhyme with a lower case letter I could have used a capital letter. Let's imagine that Kipling had a brainstorm and not only did repeat the line but added another repeated line, thus:

But there is no road through the woods;
No, there is no road through the woods
Where people can carry their goods,
Where people can carry their goods.

Because the two lines are repeated, we would describe the rhyme scheme of the new addition to the poem as follows:

A1 A1 A2 A2

Here is the rhyme scheme of a villanelle:

A1 b A2 a b A1 a b A2 a b A1 a b A2 a b A1 A2

So lines A1 and A2 are going to be the same all the way through.

Here is a villanelle by one of the compilers of this book, Mick Gowar. It is part of a much longer poem entitled *First Love*. Each section is a poem spoken by either He or She. If you want to read the whole poem, you can find it in *So Far So Good* by Mick Gowar (Penguin Poetry Plus, 1986) VI

A Few Weeks Later

She:
I don't know why, but something's going
wrong – A1
I felt the point of no return slip by. b
Though we're still happy, we still get
along A2

My heart beats like a toneless leaden
gong a
where once it leapt and raced as if to fly.
b
I don't know why. But something's going
wrong A1

in me: The spark, the naturalness has
gone a
Each day it's getting harder to deny; b
though we're still happy, we still get
along A2

I'm out of step. He hasn't changed. How
long a
each kiss feels with deceit; each touch a
lie. b
I don't know why, but something's going
wrong. A1

I'd never felt such love – so fierce and
strong: a
each sight of him, each parting made me
cry. b
Though we're still happy, we still get
along. A2
The love that was to last a whole life
through
is coming to an end. No second try,
Though we're still happy, we still get
along. A2

I don't know why, but something's going
wrong. A1

You may think that writing a poem where you keep on repeating the same line is pretty pointless and fairly easy. But no artistic form is there just for its own sake. Look carefully at the repeated lines in this villanelle and ask yourself: what effect do these repetitions have? Does the context of each repeated line as it occurs change its meaning? And what do the repetitions tell us about how the girl is feeling?

Here is another villanelle, this time by the poet Austin Dobson (1840-1921). Its title is its first line, 'When I saw you last, Rose'. However, I have jumbled the lines up and your task is to reconstruct it, using Mick Gowar's poem and the villanelle rhyme scheme as your guide. You may also find it helpful to know that the 'Rose' of the poem is both the flower and a young girl. Spotting lines A1 and A2 will be easy enough. Logic, sense, rhyme scheme and the discovery of the poem's extended metaphor will help reconstruct the rest. The final version is in the Teachers' Notes on the Assignments.

Now your petals unclose,
Yet you used not to sigh,
Like a bud ere it blows,
You were only so high:-
How fast the time goes!
When I saw you last, Rose,
In your bosom it shows
You were scarcely so shy,
How fast the time goes!
When I saw you last, Rose!
When I saw you last, Rose; –
How fast the time goes!
There's a guest on the sly;
You just peeped at the sky,
And a life, – how it grows!
When I saw you last, Rose!
Is it Cupid? Who knows!
(How fast the time goes!)
Now your Maytime is nigh; –

A final clue. Punctuation is always important – a vital clue to meaning. In Mick Gowar's poem, the punctuation of each repeated line changes and so alters its effect. Is the differing punctuation of the repeated lines in Austin Dobson's poem significant?

Probably the most famous villanelle is '*Do not go gentle into that good night*' by Dylan Thomas, where the repetitions underline and give huge force to his sense of rage at the particular death of his father and the general fact of death for everyone.

TRIOLET

Like the villanelle, the rhyme scheme is restricted to two end rhymes and whole lines are also repeated. It is eight lines long and the rhyme scheme is: A B a A a b A B.

Here, jumbled up for you to reconstruct, is Thomas Hardy's triolet *The Puzzled Game Birds*:

For did we then cry they would heed us
When we were young – they cannot be –
When we were young – they cannot be!
They are not those who used to feed us
These shapes that now bereave and bleed us
They are not those who used to feed us
– If hearts can have such treachery
They are not those who used to feed us

SONNET

Sonnets are fourteen line poems. There are two main types: The English or Shakespearian and the Italian or Petrarchan. The Shakespearian sonnet has three quatrains (four-line verses) and a couplet (a two-line verse) – though it is usually written as a single poem. The rhyme scheme is:

a b a b c d c d e f e f g g

The Petrarchan sonnet is divided in two; and eight line section, (the octet) followed by a six line section (the sestet). The rhyme scheme is:

a b b a a b b a c d c d c d

or c d e c d e

or c d e c e d

Here is a Shakespearian Sonnet (actually by Shakespeare) to reconstruct

Looking on darkness which the blind do see:
But then begins a journey in my head
For thee and for myself no quiet find.
Save that my soul's imaginary sight
For then my thoughts – from far whence I abide –
Weary with toil I haste me to my bed,
And keep my dropping eyelids open wide,
Lo! thus, by day my limbs, by night my mind,

Presents thy shadow to my sightless view,
The dear repose for limbs with travel tired
Intend a zealous pilgrimage to thee,
Makes black night beauteous and her old face new,
To work my mind when body's work's expired:
Which, like a jewel hung in ghastly night,

Remember the rhyming couplet to end. The setting out of the lines provides a clue for these. The final version is in the Teacher's Introduction to the assignments.

Here is a Petrarchan sonnet (in this case by William Wordsworth) to reconstruct. A clue for you is that the rhyme scheme in the sestet is the third of the alternatives printed above.

A sound like thunder – everlastingly.
Breathless with adoration; the broad sun
Thou liest in Abraham's bosom all the year:
Is sinking down in its tranquillity;
God being with thee when we know it not.
The gentleness of heaven broods o'er the Sea:
If thou appear untouched by solemn thought,
The holy time is quiet as a Nun
Dear Child! dear Girl! that walkest with me here,
And worship'st at the Temple's inner shrine,
Listen! the mighty Being is awake,
Thy nature is not therefore less divine:
It is a beauteous evening, calm and free,
And doth with his eternal motion make

When you have successfully finished all four of these reconstructions you will probably be feeling quite exhausted. You will have wrestled with problems of meaning as well as of form, structure and rhyme. In fact, you will have in some way experienced the struggles of the poets themselves to get these poems right; in a peculiar sort of way, by reconstructing them, you will have written them yourselves. You might be very surprised, if after the exercise you were to hide your final versions and attempt to say them from memory, how well you now know these particular poems – and also the forms they represent.

Second Stage

The aim of this activity is to give you a very specialised form of reading. In the end you will have compiled you own critical anthology of English poetry.

It is very likely that in your school's stock cupboards are old poetry anthologies which date back years and have long passed their first flush of usefulness. Get your teacher to dig some of them out so that you can use them as quarries. You are quite likely to find Vernon Scannell's *Albatross Book of English Verse* among them.

Now your aim is to make short anthologies based on form. Go through these books scanning the pages quickly to identify poems in particular forms so that you can make anthologies of them:

- An anthology of villanelles

(not easy – so aim for four at first).

- An anthology of triolets

(aim at first for five)

- An anthology of Shakespearian sonnets

(as Shakespeare wrote 154 of them, they had better be sonnets not by him – except for one of your choice)

- An anthology of Petrarchan sonnets

(Wordsworth wrote 35, so perhaps he had better be avoided as well except for one)

For both sonnet anthologies, aim for six of each type.

Third Stage

Now find definitions (perhaps in *The Albatross Book of English Verse*!) of the following:

rondeau
ballade (not ballad)
sestina

Search through the old poetry books for examples of one each of these.

Now look at larger forms. Find definitions of, and then examples of, the following;

ballad (not ballade)
epic
allegory
satire

Fourth Stage

By this time you should have compiled and edited a sizeable combined critical anthology of poetry. If the books you have used are so old as to be expendable, then scissors and paste can be used actually to make these anthologies into books of your own. If not, use of the photocopier should be allowable for all poems written by poets who are at least fifty years dead.

However, you may be quite annoyed and frustrated at the fact that, after all this emphasis on prescribed forms, identifying pure examples of some of them might prove difficult.

So, for the last activity, and the final part of your critical poetry edition:

- Find five short poems which don't seem to correspond to any form at all and try to describe them in terms of verse form and rhyme scheme.
- Hazard a guess as to why these poems are in forms peculiar to themselves and why their form has not become accepted generally.
- Write both your descriptions and your guesses down in your anthology, making it yet more of a critical work.

Fifth Stage

Now return to two of the poems with which we started this assignment – *When I last saw you, Rose* by Austin Dobson and *The Puzzled Game Birds* by Thomas Hardy; a villanelle and a triolet respectively; two very set forms indeed.

In your groups, read silently and to each other your final versions (checked against the original) until you feel there is no more that you can get out of them.

- In these poems, does the form chosen help the meaning and general effect in such a way as to make it inevitable that it should be used?

I don't know what you would have said, but in each of these poems I find the form chosen absolutely right for its purpose. The repetitions set up a sort of chiming music – and notice how what comes before and after each repeated line changes its meaning slightly every time it occurs. These two poems underline everything that the four poets interviewed have said – which is summed up by Vernon Scannell:

'… when you are using language poetically you aren't writing about something, you're actually presenting the situation itself …' and '… words have magic power … it's no accident that you never get a magic spell without it employing the techniques of poetry … if you think of language as something exciting, then you're on the way to becoming a poet.'

Your Own 'Living Writers'

Every county in England and Wales is covered by a Regional Arts Association. These are funded jointly by the Arts Board of Great Britain and the relevant local authorities. Their responsibility is to encourage the appreciation and enjoyment of the arts in their region.

As part of this responsibility, each RAA has a scheme for supporting writers' visits to schools, libraries and other groups and institutions, whereby it provides lists of recommended writers and funding to cover a proportion of the writers' fees and, in some cases, expenses. Scotland, Northern Ireland, and Eire have similar schemes which are organised through their national Arts Boards.

A wide range of activities and types of visit have been supported by RAAs in the past. These include:

- Single readings and performances;
- Single writing workshops;
- Short residencies;
- Longer residencies and residencies shared between schools or between a school and another institution such as a library or residential centre;
- Festivals and book weeks;
- Writers in in-service training courses;
- Residential writing courses for students and/or staff;
- Subscriptions to literary magazines.

The exact proportion of the writers' fees and expenses that the RAA will pay and the range of activities that it will support differs from one RAA to another. Contact the Literature Officer of your local RAA for details of its scheme. For Scotland, Northern Ireland, and Eire, contact the Literature Officer of your national Arts Board. (See page 110 for a list of addresses.)

If you want to organise a particular type of event which does not seem to be covered by the guidelines of your RAA, or you wish to book a writer who is not listed by your RAA, do not hesitate to contact the Literature Officer and discuss what you want. Not every possible type of session can be covered in their brochures and booklets and their lists are not proscriptive.

When applying for grant aid, be prepared for extra paperwork. Not only will you have to apply in writing, you will probably be asked for a short written report on the session if your application is successful. This is not bureaucratic red tape. It is vital that RAAs are able to monitor and evaluate the schemes in order to provide the best possible service for their clients.

Alternatively, if you want to involve your students in a local literature festival, contact the Literature Festivals Council, 21 Earls Court Square, London, SW5 9BY.

Organising a writer's visit

Careful preparation for a writer's visit is essential. Be clear, from the outset, exactly what your aims and objectives are and what you hope to achieve by the visit. If you are applying for financial backing from your RAA or national Arts Board, do so as early as possible. The majority of schemes receive more applications than they can support, and they do not work on the basis of the school year. They are granted funding at the beginning of the financial year (5 April), so the closer to that time that you can make your application, the greater the chance of success.

The following check-list will help you to prepare for the visit of a writer.

1 Define your aims, objectives and outcomes. What do you want the visit to achieve?

- To raise awareness/enthusiasm for literature;
- To provide specific information on a writer or a particular work;
- To encourage/improve standards of students' own writing, not just 'creative writing' but fiction, poetry, reporting, etc.;
- To encourage specific reading and/or writing skills, such as dialogue, descriptive writing, critical essays.

2 Set a possible date for the visit and contact your RAA or other funding body as far in advance as possible. Think about sources of additional or alternative funding, such as PTAs and sponsorship of local businesses or organisations. Publishers may sometimes help with costs and will provide other support, such as books, book jackets, displays, and also speakers, such as editors, to talk about publishing, book production, etc.

3 Contact the writer. Explain clearly the type of session that you want and discuss the following details:

- Date, time and location of session;
- Duration of session;
- Number, age and abilities of students involved;
- The writer's fee, and whether it is inclusive of VAT or not;
- Travel arrangements, food, and whether accommodation is needed.

Confirm all arrangements in writing.

For a workshop session, the writer may require copies of students' work before and/or after. Where possible, send copies not originals.

4 Prepare students and staff.

- Make sure that everybody knows well in advance what to expect from the session and what preparation is needed.
- Inform the local bookshop, library, press, other media, and parents about the writer's visit. This can be done by standard duplicated letter, giving brief details of the writer and his/her work, the date, time and location of the session, and the books available for sale on the day.
- Make sure that copies of the writer's work and other relevant materials are available well in advance. This may involve ordering and buying copies from normal suppliers or else borrowing from the schools' library service or local teachers' resource centre.
- Order copies of the writer's work for sale on the day of the visit through the local bookshop or schools' book shop. This can normally be done on a sale or return basis.

5 Exchange final confirmation with the writer by phone or letter.

6 Make arrangements to have ready for the writer on the day a cheque or cash for your proportion of the fee and expenses. If relevant, provide a float for the book sale.

RAAS

RAA/Arts Board
Buckingham Arts,
55 High Street, Aylesbury, Bucks HP20 1SA.

East Midlands Arts Board,
Mountfields House, Forest Road, Loughborough
Leicestershire LE11 3HU.

Eastern Arts Board,
Cherry Hinton Hall, Cherry Hinton Road, Cambridge
CB1 4DW.

London Arts Board,
3rd Floor, Elm House, 133 Longacre, London WC2E 9AF.

Yorkshire and Humberside Arts Board,
21 Bond Street, Dewsbury, West Yorkshire WF13 1AX.

North Wales Association for the Arts,
10 Wellfield House, Bangor, Gwynedd LL57 1ER.

North West Arts Board,
12 Harter Street, Manchester M1 6HY.

Northern Arts Board,
10 Osborne Terrace, Newcastle Upon Tyne NE2 1NZ.

South East Arts Board,
10 Mount Ephraim, Tunbridge Wells, Kent TN4 8AS.

S.E. Wales Arts Association,
Victoria Street, Cwmbran, Gwent NP44 3YT.

South West Arts Board,
Bradninch Place, Gandy Street, Exeter, Devon EX4 3LS.

Southern Arts,
19 Southgate Street, Winchester SO23 7EB.

W. Midlands Arts Board,
82 Granville Street, Birmingham B1 2LH.

W. Wales Association for the Arts,
Dark Gate, Red Street, Camarthen, Dyfed SA31 1QL.

Yorkshire Arts,
Glyde House, Glydegate, Bradford, Yorks BD5 0BQ.

Welsh Arts Council,
Museum Place, Cardiff CF1 3NX.

Scottish Arts Council,
19 Charlotte Square, Edinburgh EH2 4DF.

Arts Council of N. Ireland,
181a Stranmills Road, Belfast BT9 5DU.

The Arts Council, Eire,
70 Merrion Square, Dublin 2.